The Lincolnshire Poacher

David Tonge

with Abbirose Adey

Foreword
Rev Canon Alan J Robson

LadeyAdey Publications

The Lincolnshire Poacher

Copyright 2021 by David Tonge

All rights reserved. No part of this publication may be reproduced, stored in a retrieval system, or transmitted in any form or by any means—for example, electronic, photocopy, recording - without the prior written permission of the publisher. The only exception is brief quotations in printed reviews.

British Library Cataloguing-in-Publication Data.

A catalogue record for this book is available from The British Library.

ISBN: 978-1-913579-16-6 (Paperback)

ISBN: 978-1-913579-17-3 (ebook)

Publisher: Ladey Adey Publications, Copperhill, 1 Ermine Street, Ancaster, Lincolnshire, NG32 3PL, UK.

Cover Picture by Abbirose Adey of Ladey Adey Publications

Additional Copy Writing by Abbirose Adey, of Ladey Adey Publications.

Poem: *The Lincolnshire Poacher Ever After* Copyright 2021 Andrew Bowell.

The Author has done everything to ensure accreditation of copyright of other's work. The Author accepts full responsibility for any errors or omissions.

Many of the anecdotes in the book have been passed down by word of mouth, through generations and sometimes considered to be myth or folklore. The content is designed to entertain and educate. Any similarities to real people not specifically referenced is purely coincidental.

Contact the author via ceo@innovativeprimemovers.com

If you enjoyed this book, please add a review on Amazon for David.

David Tonge

This book is dedicated to
Mum and Dad
Wesley, Dawn and Charity.

"The secret of success is doing what others daren't, won't or can't."

Often said by W.E.Tonge

Celebration

We want this book to be the most comprehensive, accurate and definitive account of The Lincolnshire Poacher; the hero of the Great County of Lincolnshire - a celebration of a strategic survivialist.

If you have any stories, anecdotes, memories, newspaper cuttings and photos around the Lincolnshire Poacher, which you would like to share, please contact the author or publisher.

The Goose and the Common

The law locks up the man or woman
Who steals the goose from off the common
But leaves the greater villain loose
Who steals the common from off the goose

The law demands that we atone
When we take things we do not own
But leaves the lords and ladies fine
Who take things that are yours and mine

From a protest rhyme from 17th century England

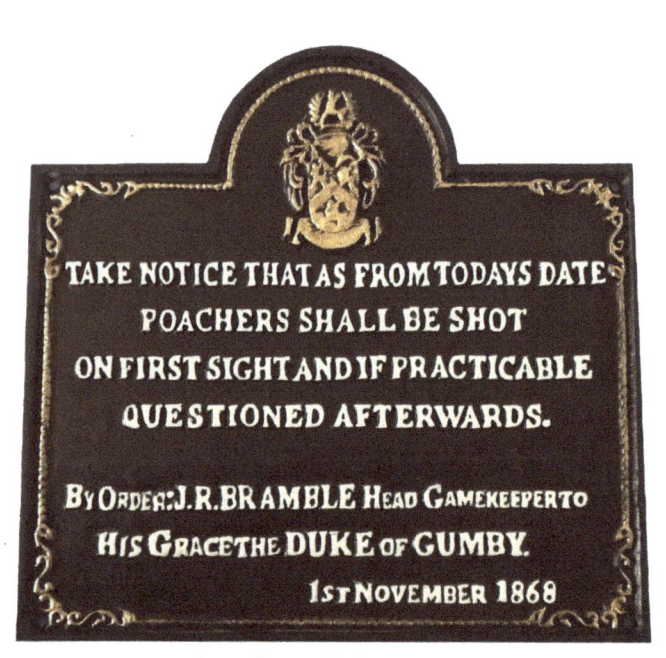

> TAKE NOTICE THAT AS FROM TODAYS DATE
> POACHERS SHALL BE SHOT
> ON FIRST SIGHT AND IF PRACTICABLE
> QUESTIONED AFTERWARDS.
>
> By Order: J.R. BRAMBLE Head Gamekeeper to
> His Grace the DUKE of GUMBY.
> 1st NOVEMBER 1868

A notice which to notice
If a poacher cares for his health.

Contents

The Lincolnshire Poacher Ever After vii
Foreword by Rev Canon Alan J Robson ix
Introduction xi
1   The Poacher's World 1
2   The Poacher's Pals 5
3   The Poacher's Tools 11
4   The Poacher's Firearms 23
5   The Poacher's Quarry 31
6   The Poacher's Remorse 43
7   The Poacher Stories 63
8   The Poacher's Parlour 79
9   The Poacher's Property 97
10 The Lincolnshire Poacher Song 105
11 The Popular Poacher 111
12 The Poacher's Glossary 115
List of Organisations 119
About the Author 125
Acknowledgements 127
References 129
Index 137

The Lincolnshire Poacher

In Genesis Chapter 25 we read, *'And Esau was a cunning hunter: a man of the field and Jacob was a plain man, dwelling in tents. And Isaac loved Esau, because he did eat of his venison.'*

So, since time began, or rather since primitive man, hunting has been an instinct. Not an instinct for pleasure, but for survival.

The eternal question is how did the families in the wilderness of Fen, Wold and Marsh survive?

The answer has resounded in my ears since I was a boy...

At dusk he emerges from the trees
His faithful pal at his heels.

The Lincolnshire Poacher Ever After

Now you've heard about my exploits
As an apprentice in Lincolnshire
And how I became a poacher
After nearly seven year
Well this new career of mine
Means living on my wits
Creeping past the big house
Where the Squire sits

>The Squire has a Gamekeeper
>A burly kind of chap
>With his bassin coat, plus-fours
>And his deerstalker cap
>He keeps trying to catch us
>And is not our biggest fan
>But we can run, skip and jump
>Faster than he can

At wine dark midnight in the wood
When the whole town is asleep
Or down by the river
Where the Willows weep
It's here you'll find the poacher
Going about his trade
With his sack, and snares and pebbles
For the catapult he's made

>Then the Poacher trudges home
>Down the woodland track
>Over the field and through the ford
>His sack slung on his back
>Nobody sees from where he comes
>Or even where he goes
>Except for the hedgehog and the fox
>The owl and the crows

So if you want a pheasant,
A rabbit or a hare
Don't ask any questions
And you really do not care
Close the curtains, lock the door
Stay inside your house
Resist the urge to take a peep
And be as quiet as a mouse

Andrew Bowell ©2021

The Lincolnshire Poacher

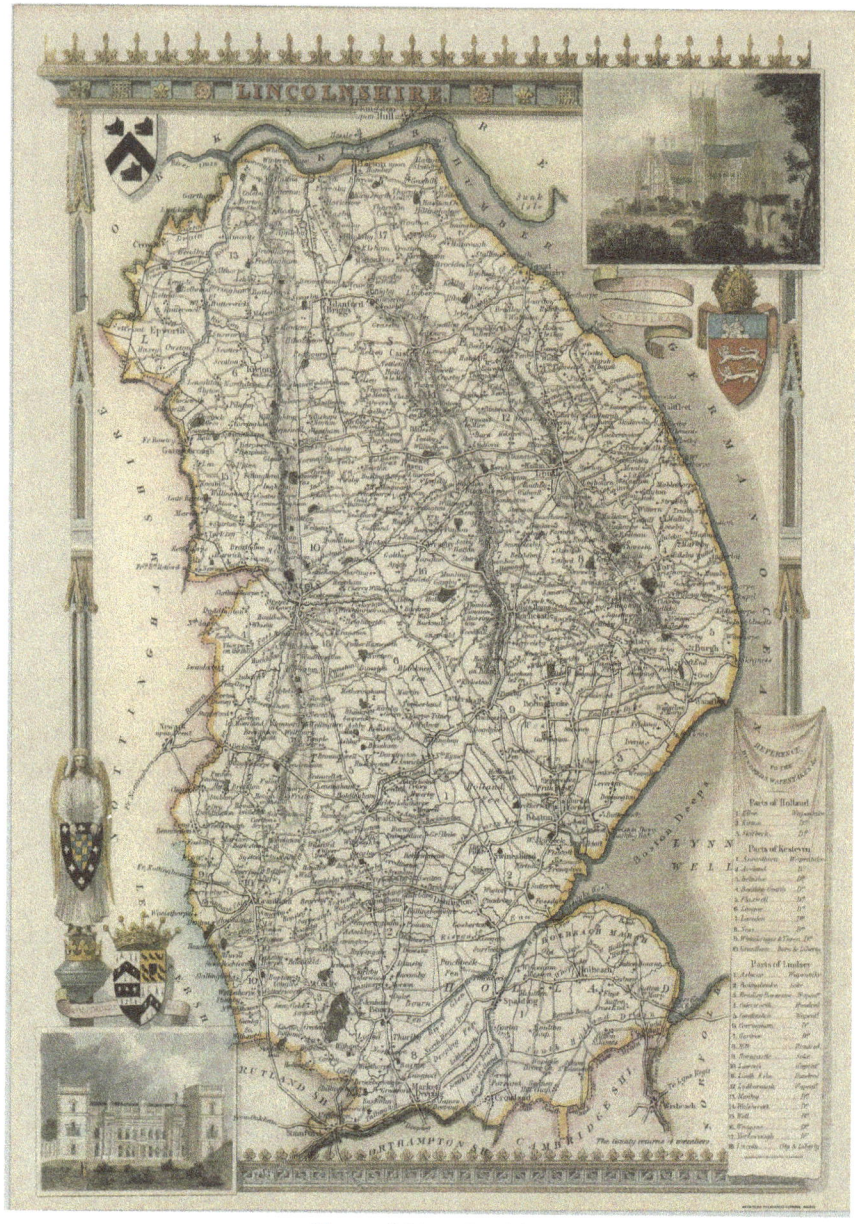

*Map of Lincolnshire
by Thomas Moule circa 1841*

Foreword

I have been the Lincolnshire Agricultural Chaplain for twenty years and have known David Tonge longer. He is a lovely chap and a kindly storyteller, you will you experience this as you read "The Lincolnshire Poacher".

David has endless interest in country ways and people. He has a self taught passion and curiosity for a wide variety of topics, not least, the dramatic changes in his beloved world of agriculture. As a smallholder and farmer in Lincolnshire, he is a 'survivor' and he has a naturally empathy for those who eke out a living from whatever they can grow or sell.

David has known all his days the Fens of Lincolnshire and has a 'home-grown' intuition to discover the curiosities and the quirky characteristics of country life.

If you, the reader, were to meet David by a country lane or in a country pub be ready for a befriending. You will have to prepare yourself for a tide of anecdotes and reminiscences - do not be in a hurry to get to your next appointment! As you listen you will get drawn into the characters, opinions and ideas that dwell in his bones. You might not agree with all you hear but David shares it with such amiability you smile and consider *'he might have a point here'*. You will not be bored or distracted. You will definitely depart from his company smiling and perhaps even wanting to explore some more avenues of interest. This little book will do this for you.

This book is a Winter's night read as you imagine *'The Lincolnshire Poacher'* embarking upon their nocturnal activities. There may be disgust at their trespass or disdain at their treatment when caught. David offers a landscape of deprivation as a legitimate background for these activities and he is not totally wrong. David hints at the power relationships between the landowners, land workers and rural people (these being skewed toward those at the top of the pecking order, who were a minority in terms of wealth). They chose to be insulated or ignore the deprivations of their neighbours and definitely their workers. David speaks into the era of the founding of the Agricultural Workers Unions of dissent and nonconformists politically and religiously.

This is David's desire, to draw us into another world and understand and learn from it, that we perhaps might understand and reflect upon how values remain but also are challenged by deprivation, disempowerment and the poverty of aspiration.

David has successfully gathered and threaded a story here for you to enjoy.

Rev Canon Alan J Robson MSc FRagS FRSA
Methodist Minister, Ecumenical Canon of Honour Lincoln Cathedral, Lincolnshire Agricultural Chaplain.

Introduction

I have always wondered why *The Lincolnshire Poacher* was called a poacher - he should have been called *The Lincolnshire Survivalist*. Traditionally, and particularly before World War One, the Lincolnshire Poacher only poached as a means for him and his family (often large families) to survive. He did not poach with the mind to send large quantities to market.

I also wonder about exactly who 'owns' the game, which freely moves from field to field, farm to farm. Game is a moving target and therefore does anyone really own it? This itself raises the question, 'Is it really poaching?' The Game Laws put through parliament by aristocratic landowners (between 1389-1831) stated that it belonged to them (qualified by estate or social standing). However, if you were a hungry farm worker, poorly paid, living in Lincolnshire 150 years ago, you would most wholeheartedly have disagreed.

The Lincolnshire Poacher

During these times, and into the mid-twentieth century, pheasants, and other game, were hunted by landowners as part of the farming economy. The large hunts allowed the rural economy to thrive. Wealthy people would pay to take part in a shoot and local country folk would be employed to work the shoot as beaters and in other roles. After the shoot, whether it was for pheasant, partridge, hare or rabbit, all the people on the estate would be given a handful of the game – much welcomed fare for hungry folk, very little was wasted.

It is important to remember back then supermarkets or shops were few or far between (nowadays it is very easy to buy a whole chicken from Tesco, Asda, Aldi, Lidl etc. for under £3.50). The people on and around the estates were self-sufficient and the shoots were a natural part of living in the countryside.

An interesting and relevant fact is: if there is an overpopulation of game, especially pheasant, they get diseased and will all die off. Official 'shoots' used to shoot hard but always left enough game to breed healthily and successfully. It was country husbandry at its finest. The poacher would have been part of this country scene – never taking more than the countryside could handle.

However, he doesn't exist in the same way anymore. He is not needed in the same way. The gut-wrenching hunger felt back then is not apparent in the same way. There is no need for people to be hungry when you can buy food more readily at the shops.

The only type of poaching that happens today is illegal hare coursing, which I wholeheartedly disagree with. These coursers are only taking part in the activity as moneymaking ventures and have no or little respect for the countryside.

Introduction

Still, I do feel it is a rite of passage, as it was for me, when a youngster in the countryside comes of age and gets their first air rifle to shoot a pheasant from their neighbour's apple tree and then take it home to have it cooked. There is a little thrill in that - a survivalist skill.

My first memory of the Lincolnshire Poacher is from when I was seven or eight. Nearby lived a poacher who used to walk down in the dyke, which was about half a mile long. By walking in the dyke he could move without being seen. The local landowner decided to dig a pit in the dyke, measuring about four foot deep. He removed all the soil and covered it with weeds - all unbeknownst to the poacher. The next time the poacher walked along the dyke - he just took a step and was up to his waist in very cold water!

As a young lad, I was always around landowners, farmers, and gamekeepers; country sports, and shooting in particular, were a first love thus the poacher was very much a part of my world. I have a few well-read books about poaching which have been influential in my understanding and fascination with him.

This fascination has led me to giving talks on him – after every talk, people want to tell me their stories about the poacher. All these wonderful anecdotes are rarely written down and often lost.

This is the main reason I felt compelled to construct this book - to share these anecdotes and all I have picked up from friends and relatives. It includes people with local knowledge, the shooting fraternity, the second-hand book stall at Melton Mowbray market (run by a very knowledgeable gentleman), retired police officers who had 'run-ins' with local poachers, retired gamekeepers and local newspapers. These are alongside the stories that my dad passed down and entrusted to me.

In addition to this list of contributors, I would also add: it has been said, '...*no book on poaching can be written without poaching information from other poaching books*'. Where possible I have referenced all the sources I have used to create my book.

Most folklore, unless passed down gets forgotten over two generations. Hopefully, this book will ensure the memory of *The Lincolnshire Poacher* continues to live on.

The good people of Lincolnshire, whether they know it or not, still have a connection with the poacher, through the very fact they were born or live here. He is synonymous with the county and seeps into our very fibre, through music, pop culture and food.

This book is for: farmers, gamekeepers and shooting enthusiasts; genealogists who wonder about lost family members; foodies who are looking for traditional poacher recipes; Yellowbellies and anyone who has (or wants) a connection to the countryside.

I hope this book entertains and educates. I challenge you to not want to know more about this legendary and well-loved character. You will feel inspired to learn more and more about him, his comical quirks and eccentricities.

1
The Poacher's World

We enter the world of the Lincolnshire Poacher 150 years ago. A time when Lincolnshire was a bleak, inhospitable, dreary place where the land was unsuitable for growing crops. Even the names of the farm reflected the miserable, and desolate situation of the environment and standards of living. For example, Hungry Hill Farm, Cold Harbour Farm, No Man's Friend Farm, Scrub Hill and Warren Farm.

There are several 'Labour in Vain' droves in the fen because they were so full of dock plants. You could stoop down and with both hands get a handful of dock seeds, making sustainable crop cultivation impossible. Incidentally, Dogdyke near Coningsby, had the original name of Dockdyke.

The Lincolnshire Poacher

Many reported the bleakness of Lincolnshire: including John Wesley, the famous Methodist preacher. He was a Lincolnshire man born in Epworth in 1703. He even found the people inhospitable. When he came to preach at Sleaford he was not well received: the crowd gathered and decided he wasn't wanted there so they pelted him with rotten fruit and vegetables.

When Wesley left he made his way to Coningsby. He had to cross the River Witham using Tattershall Bridge. At that that time, there was not a bridge; there wasn't even a ferry; it was just a crossing with big slippery stones placed in the bottom of the river. As he crossed, his horse threw him and he was soaked through, naturally this put him in a particularly bad mood. When he got to the White Bull, a pub at Coningsby (known locally at the time as the Mud and Stud due to its wattle and daub structure) he recorded in his diary, *'cold, hungry, Coningsby.'* It was a time before the industrial/agricultural drainage of the fens had taken place, and before modern fertilisers and potatoes changed the lansdscape of Lincolnshire.

Lincolnshire was sodden, crisscrossed with dykes, almost impassable. There is a little poem about North and South Kyme which goes:

Kyme God knows,
Where no corn grows
Nothing but a little hay
And the water come and takes it all away

Due to the landscape, fewer people lived in the area, but there were eel hunters, fishermen and wild fowlers. They had very large families who had to be clothed and fed.

Staving Hunger

The standard fare for folk in Lincolnshire was often dry bread and a daily mess of white sweet nettle, comfrey and boiled swede. Not an appetising or varied diet - the man of the family would have felt great pressure to provide. This is why poaching really took hold. A poacher was often friend to the very poor: many a widow with a large family, struggling to eat, would wake to find a brace of game hanging on her door.

In my Grandad's time, our hamlet of Waterside had many large families ranging from those with seven to thirteen children. If they were lucky, the family would have the old-fashioned standby - the family pig. It would be well fed and well cared for, slaughtered at the end of harvest to last them through the winter and beyond. The pig was most likely to be a Lincolnshire Curly Coat, weighing up to 30 stone.

This was not so much meat pig, as a lard pig (my mum used to call them '*Lard on Legs*'). The fat in the pig was more prized than the meat in these hard times. Lard has come and gone out of fashion - but what goes around comes around. One of the bestselling recipe books in the USA is: *Lard: The Lost Art of Cooking with Your Grandma's Secret Ingredient!* The pig was the bedrock of survival, but once it was eaten, what did you do?

The Lincolnshire Poacher

William Cobbett, an English journalist, agriculturalist and political reformist, stated in his book, *Rural Rides*, '...*the keeping of pigs by cottages was a matter of moral and political emancipation; a couple of flitches of bacon are worth 50,000 Methodists sermons and religious tracks. The sight of them on the rack tends to keep a man from poaching and stealing than an old volume of penal statutes though assisted by the terror of deportation and the gibbert.*'

Cobbett understood that if families had access to food they were far less likely to poach. As it was they were starving and they knew that outside their cottages, the fields were crawling with game.

Getting that game without anybody knowing lay the ancient art and craft of poaching. A Lincolnshire tradition by that most romantic of characters, Lincolnshire's most native son celebrated in song and legend - *The Lincolnshire Poacher.*

*Full well I served my master
For more than seven year.*

2
The Poacher's Pals

A poacher's life was a difficult and lonely one. He would have worked alone, never quite trusting anyone and possibly on the outskirts of society. However, he had a few trusted companions on whom he could rely on for company and more importantly to help him in his *'shady dealings'*.

The Poacher's Dog

Ideally, a dog needed to be small so he could almost be carried in a pocket, like a Norfolk Terrier or Border Terrier. It could legitimately be kept on the farm to keep down the population of rats, mice and rabbits. This type of dog would be ideal for taking a brace of rabbits from the local warren.

This photo of 'Lord *Billy the Hat* Barton' was taken at a Woodhall Spa 1940s weekend.

He always comes dressed as *'The Lincolnshire Poacher'*, despite being a Yorkshireman!

Lying in wait, the poacher and his dog would be patient, on lookout for rabbits leaving a warren. A warren was often a man-made affair, always built on sandy soil or a silt hill where it was easy for the rabbits to burrow and breed. On top of the warren, you would put the hedge trimmings and old tree roots - heaping them up to provide cover for the rabbits to breed safely. Most farms had a warren, and it is reported that in the disastrous depression of the 1930s some farms in Norfolk were only saleable if they had a warren.

In addition to the small stature of the dog, the poacher preferred a dog of reddish colour. A dog with this colouring is actually a lure to game itself. This is linked to a phenomenon known as 'protean behaviour'. This is where prey is attracted to or displays behaviour that creates a 'fight' response rather than flight. Foxes are a natural red colour, and as foxes are predators of the prey also preferred by poachers, it is clear birds respond to red dogs as they would a fox. It has been noticed throughout the ages and I personally have seen this behaviour twice, where birds have tried to 'mob' a dog. Reddish dogs also make great 'decoy dogs' mentioned in Chapter 3 - The Poacher's Tools. The word Protean comes from the Greek 'Proteus'. He was a sea god that could change his shape unexpectedly to avoid capture.

The Poacher's Pals

Other than matching the colour and size of the dog, the poacher would also attempt to create the perfect dog to assist in his task, known in Lincolnshire as 'a longdog'. Sometimes referred to as 'lurchers', not to be mistaken with a Norfolk Lurcher, which was more brindle in colour. The Lincolnshire Longdog was held in high esteem by the people of the county. Still to this day there are buildings named after this respected hound. This is not a specific 'breed of dog' but a carefully selected and bred type of dog - one that could hunt, jump, kill and carry. It also required speed, stamina, strength and good sight.

To acquire these characteristics in one dog, it had to be carefully bred, so that these traits came out. For speed, the poacher needed a Saluki and he crossed it with a Bedlington for stamina. The resulting offspring was ready for crossing with the offspring of a Smithfield-Drover (for its strength). This breed was like a big bearded collie, sadly a breed now extinct. This was then crossed with a Greyhound, for its sight. The offspring of this final cross was the true longdog of the Poacher; a dog for dark nights to let slip and roam the stubble fields for hare and rabbit. It was banned on most farms and estates.

You could be sent to prison or deported to Australia for owning a dog such as this but the risk was often taken, as the Lincolnshire Longdog was the ultimate meat-harvesting machine!

Even though the Smithfield-Drover is extinct in Europe, some were taken to Australia to use on their sheep and cattle stations. It was not a success in the main, as it was too hot for them, however some enterprising shepherds took them to Tasmania, a much cooler part of Australia, bred them and used them with great success. Subsequently, there is now a dog called the Tasmanian Smithfield-Drover!

In old colour paintings of the Poacher and his dog, the dog is often shown as a red and white setter.

The Poacher's Ferret

Another animal favoured by the poachers was the ferret. Often he would breed his own out in his back garden, handling them every day, so they became very tame. He could carry them out in his pocket and just nip them down a rabbit hole for them to bolt into his nets. His favourite type of ferret was a Polecat, larger than normal ferret. Technically, it was a cross between a ferret and a Pine Martin. Most of the old hands knew these as 'Foul Martins'. They were like a skunk, when disturbed or protecting themselves they gave off a foul smell.

The Poacher's Cat

All farm houses and farmyards had various cats of all colours, crosses and shapes. They were used for vermin control, particularly of rats and mice, before rodenticides were invented.

The poacher would have a cat living in his cottage but as there was no such thing as bought cat food; cats had to fend for themselves. At night, they would be put out to go hunting in the surrounding countryside. Sometimes, when you opened the door in the morning on the mat could be a rat, rabbit, partridge or even a pheasant.

Gamekeepers were particularly annoyed if this happened out of season and if the pheasant was a hen. If it was a nesting hen, it potentially meant a clutch of eggs would then not hatch,

We had a farm cat who at various times brought in pheasants and fully-grown rabbits. On one occasion, it brought in a live kingfisher. When the cat let it go, I had never seen a bird fly so fast!

The Lincolnshire Poacher

*And taking on 'em up again,
We caught a hare alive.*

3
The Poacher's Tools

Before the Lincolnshire fens and marshes were drained, they were teeming with many varieties of ducks, geese and other waterfowl. It is said, that in spring, you couldn't walk more than 10 yards in any direction without putting your foot on a duck's nest. When quietly walking about in the Fens, if you took a pot shot at a bird all the birds took flight. It was as though the fen itself was actually taking off.

The poacher would often observe gamekeepers and landowners, he would learn and reproduce techniques he saw them use, plus use their resources if he could. An essential technique he would have observed and utilised would have been the usage and protocols of Duck Decoys.

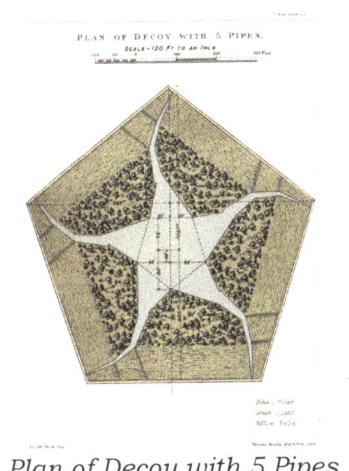

Plan of Decoy with 5 Pipes Sir Ralph Frankland-Payne-Gallwey

Duck Decoys

To harvest this plethora of ducks and geese, structures were built to trap them, called duck decoys. Some were in the shape of the old three penny bit (octagonal), while others were in the shape of a pentagon. They had spider dykes coming from each corner, willow trees growing at the side, a large patch of water positioned in the centre, all netted, and the idea was to attract all the ducks into this trap.

To get the ducks attention, using their understanding of protean behaviour our ancestors bred a special type of dog, small (about the size of a modern day cocker spaniel), which had two qualities: i) its red-fox colouring and ii) its erratic behaviour. Ducks and geese have a primeval fear of the red fox and they would often attack the fox-like dog moving about.

Decoyman Enticing Wild Ducks Up The Decoy Pipe By The Use Of A Dog Sir Ralph Frankland-Payne-Gallwey

The local hunters used this as a way to fool the ducks into entering the decoy. This was done very successfully all over the region. It is thought Lincolnshire had more duck decoys than any other county, forty known in total. I once came across a very old bloke who called Lincolnshire '40 'Coy', I have never heard anyone else call it that before or since. Today, I know two local farmers, each with red-coloured Border Terriers, when shooting on their farms, they have noticed when ducks fly over they sometimes try to 'dive bomb' the dogs.

The duck decoy was a successful money spinning operation. The ducks were sent down to London for the meat, but the feathers and down were left in Lincolnshire and sent to Fogarty's in Boston and Billingborough. It is an urban legend (or country legend) that one year, using only one decoy, enough ducks were caught, sold for meat and feathers - made enough to buy a for 700-acre farm - paid for in cash - we're talking big money!

The poacher, knowing the money to be made from selling ducks for meat and their plumage, always made sure that one of his dogs was a red-coloured terrier-spaniel cross (using aforementioned observed techniques). As he went about, his dog could often attract a brace of ducks into shotgun range.

Sadly, the red Decoy Dog as a breed became extinct with the drainage of the Fens and the arrival of more powerful sporting guns, discussed in Chapter 4 - The Poacher's Firearms.

Guile and Cunning

To get an elusive pheasant into his game-bag, the poacher had to use guile and low native cunning. One of his favourite tricks would be to start feeding pheasants at the corner of the field or at the side of the wood. He would cut off the corners of thick blue paper sugarbags (some of you may be old enough to remember these), coat the insides of the corners with birdlime (an old form of *super glue* made from boiled holly leaves) and sprinkled with grain, then pressed down into the ground. When the cock pheasant came along and pecked into this corner of the bag, it stuck to his head like a hat. He would immediately crouched down in fear and stay there. The poacher just had to walk along, pick it up and wring its neck.

Drunken Birds

Another way to catch them was to find a bird's regular feeding place, feed them raisins soaked in rum or brandy. This would make them drunk and easy to run down.

Pea and Horsehair

The poacher would also use a pea and horsehair technique. For this, they needed a pea and a two-foot length of horsehair from a horse's mane or tail. Carefully, he would make a hole in the middle of the pea, without breaking it, then thread the horsehair into the middle and tie it there. He would make several of these and throw them down where the pheasants were feeding. The pheasant would eat one of these, swallow it, so the pea would be in its stomach, but the horsehair would be sticking out of its mouth. The pheasant would wear itself out by trying to get the hair out of its mouth and eventually when it was exhausted, the poacher could just pick it up.

Fuming

On a lovely, still night if there were half a dozen pheasants roosting in a tree, the poacher would get an old, empty treacle can and fill it half full with flowers of sulphur and a little bit of tinder and light it. The lid of the tin (previously perforated) fixed on top and the tin under the tree. The fumes would rise with heat and the pheasants would fall down unconscious.

There are also rumours that some poachers used stilts to pick the roosting cock pheasants out of the trees, but I've no hard evidence to prove this.

The Poacher's Tools

Knitting Needles and Hat Pins.

If a pheasant was perched low down in a large tree, a poacher could use a long hazel pole and fasten a sharpened knitting needle or hatpin to it. They would stand underneath the pheasant carefully putting the pole up towards it. When close enough, one quick stab in its chest would kill the bird. This would have taken patience and stealth.

Snare

The poacher's most popular tool was the snare, a copper wire often put in hedgerows and dyke sides to catch rabbits, but it would sadly catch other things as well.

All he had to do was to find a rabbit run through a hedge or dyke side, peg the snare down and come back the next day to pick up the dead rabbit. It was a criminal offence to be carrying snares on someone else's land with the intention of poaching, so the poacher found ingenious ways of carrying the snares so that no one else could tell. His most favourite way was to put them under his shirt collar. Consequently, whenever the police caught a poacher, they would always check this first. This is how the phrase, '*We felt his collar!*' came about.

Catapult

The old poachers always carried a self-built catapult, which was silent and deadly on close range game. On YouTube, you can find several clips of men using catapults to hunt game with remarkable success. Have a look and you will be well and truly surprised.

Shutknife

Another tool the Poacher always carried was a shutknife (or penknife), often made in Sheffield by IXL or Taylors Eyewitness. It was sometimes known as 'a lambsfoot' knife. There is old saying, '...*the staghorn handle and lambsfoot blade was the finest cutting edge that was ever made.*' Razor sharp and paper-thin blades would gut a rabbit, whittle a peg for a snare, or cut a willow slip to make an eel trap.

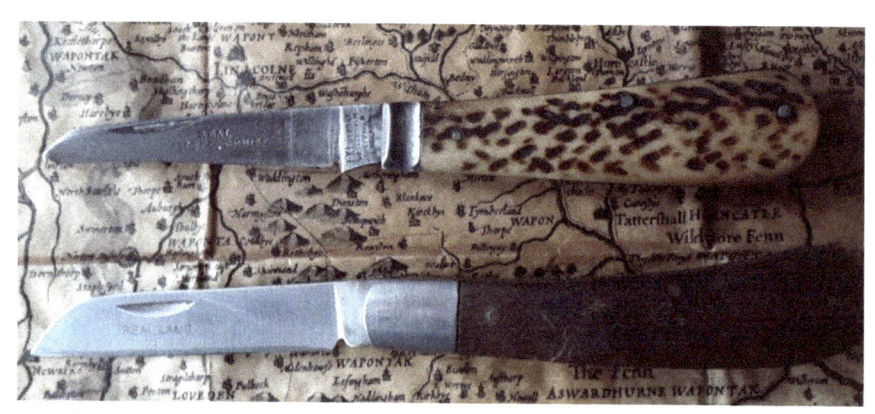

The staghorn handle was warm to the touch on the coldest night and its rough texture was great for gripping with frozen fingers. The Sheffield design was considered the best as the more it was used the better it got. The poacher would sharpen the blade on his stone doorstep, making it thinner and sharper over time.

Pole Vault

In a hard Winter with the water frozen over it was possible to walk across the Fenlands of Lincolnshire. Remember they were criss-crossed by dykes, drains, forty foots and twenty foots, creeks, delphs, catch waters, flumes and sewers, sluices, skeriths, becks, brooks, wash dykes, fodder dykes, meers, eau dykes and sykes lo 'oles. However, the rest of the year the poacher had to rely on his ingenuity. One solution was to pole vault. An ash pole about 2 inches thick and 14 foot long was needed for the pole. The poacher would have several of these collected up over the summer months. Whenever he saw a suitable trunk growing in the woods he would cut it down and save it.

These poles would be hidden in strategic places so he could use them in his forays across the fen; mostly hiding them in a ploughed furrow or the huvver of the dyke side, poked into the grass where only the poacher knew it was hidden.

With his folding .410 in his inside jacket pocket and his game bag on his back he could pole vault across the dykes and soon get several miles to a covert where the pheasants were roosting.

Many landowners and gamekeepers thought the pheasants were safe and out of the way of the poachers because of the security of deep dykes and drains, never realising that the wily old poacher had a trick or two up his sleeve. It is surprising how wide a stretch of water you can pole vault over and how springy an ash pole can be when you are at the very end of it. The poacher would have to vault at a run before the pole sunk too deeply in the mud else he would be left stranded in the air.

When the Poacher was on his way back with a bag full of poached pheasants, he would throw them across the dyke and then pole vault himself over. Definitely an art!

Traps

There were a number of traps available and a poacher would choose the most suitable. They were however, easy to spot by a watchful keeper. If found in possession of a trap the poacher would have found it quite tricky to explain why they had it!

A *'gin-trap'* ranged in size and could be used to catch anything from the tiny kingfisher, to large predators, this included humans - notably a *'man-trap'*, discussed more in Chapter 6 - The Poacher's Remorse.

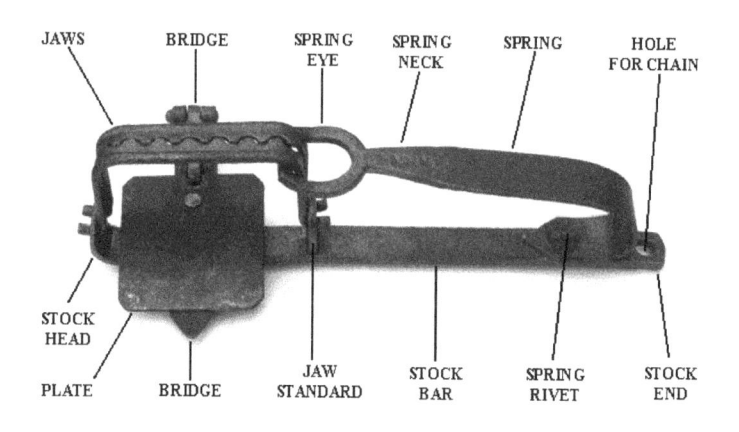

JAWS BRIDGE SPRING EYE SPRING NECK SPRING HOLE FOR CHAIN

STOCK HEAD
PLATE BRIDGE JAW STANDARD STOCK BAR SPRING RIVET STOCK END

A *'gin-trap'* generally refers to a spring operated mechanical device, with or without 'teeth', designed to catch an animal by the leg or head. The term *'gin'* is believed to have come from the word *'engine'* used for centuries to describe any mechanical device.

They also included *'pole-traps'* specifically created to catch birds of prey, as they would land on poles (hence the name). The poacher wouldn't use a pole-trap particularly, but his enemy, the gamekeeper, may have as these birds would naturally kill and feed on game birds.

Netting

There were many types of net that the poacher would have used. These would have ranged from the *'long-net'*, a *'gate-net'*, a *'trail-net or trammel-net'* to a small *'rabbiting-net'*.

Long-netting

Long-netting was a real rabbit money earner but required a gang (minimum of three) and preferably a dog to sweep the area. Each net would be about a hundred yards long and up to six could be set. The net mesh was made to exact dimensions so the rabbit would get its head through but not out again. Besides needing a large number of people to coordinate a netting operation (including the butchering afterwards), the main disadvantage to long-netting was ensuring the correct folding and storage of the nets. If they were tangled they could not be set easily or silently.

Trail-netting

Trail-nets were more likely to be used for partridge poaching. They were often between twelve and fifteen feet long with a hazel pole at each end. With a man at each end, the net would be trailed along the field, brushing the ground behind. Trail-netting took a lot of advanced watching in preparation for the actual occasion. Looking for stubbles where the covey would have *'jugged'* for a night and piles of droppings. Patience and keen observation skills were essential traits for a successful poacher to possess.

Gate Net

A straight forward net which only needed to be as wide as the gate when stretched across. It was a net often used in hare poaching. A hare prefers to leave a field the way in which it entered. If a poacher had observed a popular hare run he may have been able to learn which entry the hare preferred. On spotting a hare entering a field via his normal route, the poacher would be able to stretch a gate net across the hare's point of entry, then scare the hare back the way it came, hopefully straight into his net.

Rabbiting Net or Purse Net

A rabbiting net was shaped like a bag, or purse. The mouth of the net could be drawn together with cords and was mainly used to catching rabbits, although it was also good for catching fish. This type of net was placed over a rabbit hole and would catch any rabbit attempting to escape the poacher's ferret. Due to its small size it was easy to conceal and it was a convenient way to carry any caught game back home.

Rabbiting Spade

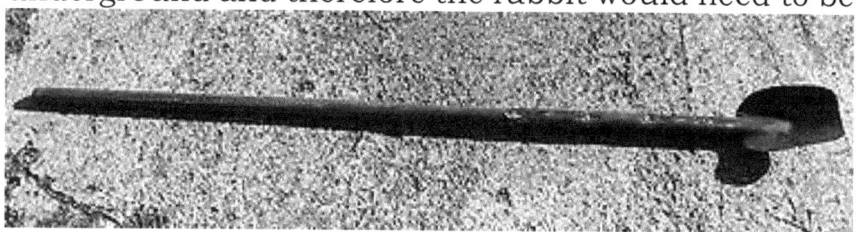

A rabbiting spade had a wooden handle and a narrow metal blade with a curved end. The poacher would have taken it out with him if he used ferrets for rabbiting. Sometimes, the ferret would kill the rabbit underground and therefore the rabbit would need to be dug out. Other times, the ferret would gorge himself on the rabbit, and settle down to sleep, in which case the poacher needed to dig out the ferret! Some poachers may have muzzled or even sewn the jaws of the ferret together to stop either situation from happening.

Bird Calls

The poacher would generally work in silence wherever possible, yet it would sometimes be necessary to recreate a call to entice his unsuspecting prey. Sometimes the poacher would know the different calls each prey made and what each call meant, such was his connection with nature. However, sometimes he would have needed the aid of a bird call, sometimes known as a bird whistle, to recreate a call. There were a wide variety of different whistles available. The poacher may have even made his own out of easily accessible (and explainable) materials, such as bone or horn.

The Lincolnshire Poacher

*'Twas when we spied the gamekeeper
For him we did not care.*

4
The Poacher's Firearms

As weapons progressed it is natural that the poacher moved along with the times - he was after all a survivalist. The first firearms to be introduced were muzzle-loaders. Single barrelled 12 bore hammer guns with 32 inch barrels. Soon cartridges came in and breach loading guns became standard, as they were easier to use. Despite having a long range for a shotgun, they were not ideal for the poacher as they were very noisy and difficult to conceal.

The weapon of choice for the dedicated poacher was one that could be easily hidden: inside a jacket, at the front of a waistcoat, down a trouser leg or slipped into a long pocker and hidden by your arm as you held it in place.

The Lincolnshire Poacher

The ideal gun was the folding .410 gauge, the 'derringer' of shotguns. It was cheap, small, light, handy with very little recoil and was quiet.

In addition to the physical concealment aspect of his clothing, the poacher had an undergarment of sheepskin called a pelt to keep him warm. He would sometimes use the sleeve to stop his hand freezing on the bare metal barrel. This had the bonus element that it quieted the noise of the gun.

The .410 gauge shot guns were once a common sight in the catalogues of British gun makers, though they were not generally made in Britain. In the late 1890s to 1950s, they were made in large quantities, tens of thousands, and were mostly unmarked (lacking makers signs, or numbers to

identify them). They mostly chambered for the original 2" .410 cartridge but sometimes they were chambered for the 2.5" four long.

'The price was £2.00, which at the time would have bought you four hundred Eley .410 cartridges. That, in today's money, would be akin to buying the gun for £123.00. An agricultural labourer made £1.10s. 8d per week in 1932 so the gun represented about one and a half week's wages. Grade 4 agricultural pay in 2019 was £320 per week.'

So, the little Belgian .410 represented the kind of outlay a modern Yildiz does for an agricultural labourer today' (Vintage Gun Journal, 1st December 2019).

Forget about your Purdey's, Churchill's, Boss's or Holland & Holland's, this is the gun that has shot more game, legal or illegal, than anything other. Consequently, it has probably saved many marriages, quieted hungry kids and kept the underground rural economy moving.

In the Vintage Gun Journal, the young countryman is challenged not to feel a tingle of excitement as a latent poacher after restoring one of these old .410 shotguns. They also suggest that restoration of such a gun is a great project for a beginner restorer and shooter.

Some of the poachers returning from both World Wars brought back their Lee Enfield .303 rifles. It is often said that *'a soldier's best friend is his rifle'* and therefore a rifle held great sentimental value to each soldier thus many men did not surrender them when demobilised. However, a .303 rifle was no good for shooting game. A well-reputed firm of gun-makers, Elderkins, based in Spalding, specialised in re-boring and was able to convert .303s into .410s. These were very reliable, hard hitting guns and fired a magnum 3" cartridge, a bit noisy with a bolt action. However, they were also heavy and could not be folded or hidden so easily, ultimately making them less popular for the poacher. These are now very collectable and fetch good money.

Here is an advert for Elderkins Special Magnum .410 Shotguns, a converted rifle that was incredibly popular.

SPECIAL MAGNUM .410 SHOTGUNS

We proudly announce and can offer with complete confidence, a very special line in .410 shotguns.

A great deal of thought and research has gone into the production of this revolutionery type of gun that we are offering to sportsmen who appreciate a really hard hitting, long range, safe, reliable, single shot .410.

Manufactured from the well designed and finely made .303 bolt action service rifle, known to many tens of thousands of British servicemen during World War II, this has now been developed into a soundly constructed bolt action, single shot .410 shotgun, which will give a lifetime's reliable service to the British farmer and sportsman.

This weapon was designed to stringent Government specifications for strength and reliability. Each weapon has been completely stripped, the rifling removed, the barrel bored, and very carefully polished to take .410 cartridges, and is made of highest quality steel, bored fullest possible choke and chambered to take 3" EXTRA LONG MAGNUM .410 CARTRIDGES, as well as the standard length ammunition (2½" FOURLONG and 2" FOURTEN). The MAGNUM 3" cartridge contains 11/16 oz. of shot which is almost a 20 bore load, and for shooting at ranges up to 40 yards.

Each shotgun has been individually nitro proved at the BIRMINGHAM GUN BARREL PROOF HOUSE AND NO FIREARM CERTIFICATE IS NECESSARY. By virtue of the 25" full choke barrel and being able to use a Magnum cartridge, a very dense pattern can be obtained at extreme ranges. This gun is unsurpassed by any other .410 for long distance killing. The very safe bolt mechanism is silk smooth and superior in every way, also readily detachable for ease in cleaning.

Weight approx 6¼lbs.

Cartridges sent CARRIAGE PAID with gun order. The above weapons can be fitted with eyes and strong leather sling at additional cost

Very strong canvas cover with sling to fit magnum .410, or without sling.

Two piece .410 cleaning rod and three attachments, also .410 one piece steel rod with brush and loop.

EXTRA LONG 3" MAGNUM CARTRIDGES, shot sizes (3, 4, 5, 6, 7, shot)

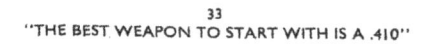

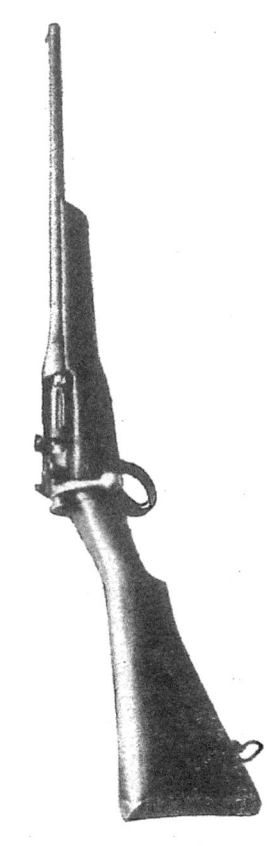

33
"THE BEST WEAPON TO START WITH IS A .410"

This gun was so good that when the supply of them came to an end, Webley & Scott of Birmingham started to make a copy of them.

> # experience the 'feel' of a Webley ·410 – it's built to last
>
> The moment you pick it up you will see that the Webley ·410 bolt action is beautifully made from top-class materials, and at a very reasonable price. Every single part of this wonderful little gun is sturdy — yet it is light and easy to handle. Examine the finish and see just how much detailed work goes into making this Webley the best buy in single barrel ·410's.
>
> Specification: Barrel length 25½". Modified choke. 2½" chamber. Bead foresight. Bolt fitted with double bite and cam which holds striker nose clear of bolt face until bolt is closed as added safety measure. Extractor — half moon, anchored to prevent loss. Stock — standard model fitted with good quality beech stock, not chequered. Length 14¼". Weight — 5¼ lb. Safety device — manual. Cartridge Recommended Fourlong with No. 5 or No. 6 shot. The De Luxe model has a walnut stock, is hand chequered and polished, and is fitted with a heel plate. Prices from £12.13.0.
>
> **WEBLEY** Buy the Webley ·410 from your local gun stockist or write for illustrated literature of this and other Webley guns to:—Dept. ST/EG3, Webley & Scott Ltd. (Incorporating W. W. Greener Ltd.), Park Lane, Handsworth, Birmingham 21. Tel: 021-553 3952.

Cartridges

If you needed to kill something bigger than a pheasant or goose, e.g. a sheep, pig, or deer, you needed a cartridge and you could do one of two things. You could open the crimp at the top and drop some molten candle wax in so it fused the pellets together as a sold projectile. This would kill large game, but only if you fired it in a shotgun which wasn't choked - if it was choked, it would kill you.

You could also use a knife around the cartridge between the shot and the powder to cut a perforation mark all around the paper casing, so that when you fired, the whole of the pellet case, including the wadding, came out as a projectile.

There were other things which could put in place of shot in the cartridges. Sometimes the poacher added rock salt, so he could shoot sitting pheasants without blowing them to pieces and with no marks on them. This is what the USA law enforcement use as a *'riot round'* to fetch rioters and terrorists off buildings without doing too much damage. It stings, but by the time they are examined by the medics, there is not much to see.

Mark Twain, in one of his musings, tells us that when he was *'out west'*, celebrating with a few drinks, he and a gang of friends got up on the roof of the saloon to party. As they were making merry and causing a commotion, the local Sheriff was called for. As they would not obey his command to come down, two rounds of rock salt was fired at their legs from a double barrelled 12 bore, which got them down immediately!

A friend of mine, Neil Mablethorpe, a blacksmith in Walcott, told me a tale of an acquaintance of his; one Edwin Skinner of Martin. He farmed in the dip of the back road between Timberland and Martin He kept pigs and lived off the land (including game that wandered around the area). Later on in his life, he had to go to hospital for a scan and the number of lead pellets in his stomach surprised the doctor.

The hospital wanted to call the police on the understanding that he had been shot, but Edwin told them that all his life he had eaten pheasants and the shot had come from them!

One safer replacement for lead shot was '*tic- beans*'. These are small beans beloved by the pigeon fanciers. The poacher would soak them in vinegar and cook them in the oven to make them very hard (in the same way children do with conkers) The great thing about this type of round is no breaking of teeth when eating pheasant as the bean shot would dissolve in the cooking process - very much welcomed by some of the poacher's '*customers*'.

The Lincolnshire Poacher

*We took him to a neighbour's house
And sold him for a crown.*

5
The Poacher's Quarry

The poacher would go out as and when needed and different times of year would dictate what quarry would be most available and most profitable. He also needed weather conditions to be favourable.

The best pheasant poaching weather conditions were often when a gale was howling. This was when the pheasants would sit tight. Obviously, a real moonlit night wasn't the best time to poach (despite what the song claims) as it would be easy to see the poacher, shadows could form easily and if crossing a ridgeline a clear silhouette would be seen.

The colder the weather was, the better it was for poaching. How did the Poacher tell it was cold enough, you ask? Remember, he lived in an old cottage, with no central heating and no double glazing. He knew if the contents of the chamber pot under the bed had frozen over, it was the ideal night for a bag full of pheasants, rabbits or a hare!

Rabbits

Rabbits are not a native species to the UK. We have to thank the Normans for bringing them over during the Conquest. However, we could consider them *'an illegal immigrant who has done remarkably well'*.

Even the Bible mentions the success of the survivability and adaptability of rabbits, rabbits here are referred to as 'conies' or 'coneys'.

*'The coneys, a species with little power,
yet they make their home in the rocks;'*
Proverbs 30 V 26 (CJB)

*'The high hills are a refuge for the
wild goats; and the rocks for the conies.'*
Psalm 104 V18 (KJB)

Pre-myxomatosis, it is believed there were 50 million rabbits in the United Kingdom - eating four times the amount the national sheep flock ate. One of the places they overran was a small village in central Lincolnshire - there were so many rabbits it was named after them - Coningsby! Lincoln Heath has been described by a Miss S Hatfield as *'a moving plain of a busy republic of rabbits'*. Surely a paradise for the poacher? Before myxomatosis, rabbits were bigger, stronger and meatier and lived underground. When food rationing finished in this country after the war, about the same time that myxomatosis decimated the rabbit population; the experts reckoned there was an extra £52 million worth of food for the population to eat now the rabbits were gone.

The Poacher's Quarry

Is it coincidence that rationing and the decimation of rabbits happened at the same time?

Old paintings of rabbit hunting show the shooters carrying their *'bag'* containing bigger rabbits. Despite Victorian artists exaggerating their subjects it is thought the creatures would certainly have been a bigger animal than today, especially on the heaths and the Wolds. However, in the fens and marshes they may have been significantly smaller because they would have used so much energy to keep warm hindering growth.

There were two distinct types of rabbit. The Common Grey: which was used for meat and the more rare Silverback: which was used for clothes and hats. The Silverbacks were worth considerably more and the majority of them were skinned and shipped down to London for the millinery business. Lincolnshire on the Wolds was famous for its Silverbacks - a prize well worth poaching. Louth Park was reputed to be the place where the best Silverbacks were found. It is recorded that keepers often released a few coloured (black or white) rabbits into managed warrens to discover whether poaching was occuring. If any of these black or white rabbits disappeared suspicions were aroused and a watch kept.

An experience poacher however, would have avoided taking these colourful inhabitants. The Silverback (or Silver-grey as it is sometimes known) is traditionally associated with Lincolnshire although there is some contention to where they originated from. The author Oliver Goldsmith believed they originated from an island in the Humber estuary, but according to tradition the Silver-grey was brought over from Ireland.

There is a famous court case where a gang of lads aged between 12 and 14 years old were out for a lark and were caught poaching Silverback rabbits at Louth Park. They were arrested, taken to court and charged accordingly. The cruel aristocratic judge wanted to make an example of them and sentenced them to seven years hard labour and transportation to Australia.

There was a huge outcry, as the parents and relatives of the lads knew that they would never see them again.

The story then continues in folklore with an aunt of one of these lads, who unbeknown to the Judge, got a job as a cook in his household and over the next 18 months got him used to spicier than normal food and slowly poisoned him to death. She got away with it, and those in the know thought this was 'proper justice'. Incidentally, there is now a very prosperous community founded by these lads from Lincolnshire called 'Louth Park' in Maitland, New South Wales, Australia.

In the 18th century only a few people were allowed to kill rabbits, but there was one piece of land where an exception was made: on the sea-defences of South Lincolnshire. Rabbits caused so much damage to the sea-banks an Act of 1765 permitted any man to kill

[43 & 44 VICT.]   Ground Game Act, 1880.   [CH. 47.]

CHAPTER 47.
An Act for the better protection of Occupiers of Land against injury to their Crops from Ground Game. A.D. 1880.
[7th September 1880.]

them on land up to one furlong from the estuaries. Unquestionably, a boon for the poacher in this area! In 1880, another Act came into being: The Ground Game Act which enabled landowners, occupiers and any person authorised in writing to kill rabbits (in the daytime). There were a number of weaknesses in the Act which landowners were quick to exploit, thus adversely affecting the poacher again.

It is often a surprise to me that poachers were condemned for poaching rabbits as they were often a pest to landowners and occupiers. In Lincolnshire during the late 18th and early 19th centuries, landowners were expected to create subdivisions of pastures. Hedge-planting was a popular choice but rabbits were a horrid nuisance causing *'damage to young quick-set hedges'*. I am sure if the poachers had been allowed to collect rabbits much of this destruction could have been avoided. In addition to this, most poachers would make no money from the theft of rabbits, only the butcher would have lost out here - *'a rabbit saved a family from having to buy a small joint at the weekends'*.

Hare

Lincolnshire has the largest native hare population density in the country, which makes it very popular with the coursing fraternity.

The hare is often described as *'an animal of mystery'*, and is under stress from the reintroduced birds of prey such as: buzzard, red kites and hen harriers, which kill and eat the young leverets. So-called conservationists and environmentalists who campaigned for this reintroducion do not fully understand the balance of nature and the impact this action has had.

Hare is a dark, strong, meat of which one animal could feed a large family (approximately 6 - 8 people).

Every game cookbook talks about *'Jugged Hare'* but I don't know anyone who cooks it this way, especially not with the blood and vinegar. This would be particularly true in Lincolnshire a predominantly Methodist county. The Methodist's biblical instruction is to not drink blood, but rather pour the blood on the ground and used for fertiliser; not cooking.

Partridge

'One bird – one man- one meal!' This quote references the Old English variety of partridge (not the French variety aka 'Red Leg'). The partridge is not a bright bird but is the best tasting of all game.

Plate 143 - Partridges
A.W. Seaby

It is always found in coveys and is probably the UK's only genuine native game bird - a true example of Great British wildlife (often seen on the sides of country lanes after the road grit).

A good sign of the health of a farm and countryside is the number of partridge covey populations. If they start disappearing, it is the same as canaries dropping off their perches down the pit – not a healthy sign!

Duck

We have already discussed the prominence of duck in Chapter 3 - The Poacher's Tools, but it needs to be mentioned here too, as it was ready game for the poacher.

Plate 158 - Mallard: Two Drakes pursuing a Duck
A.W. Seaby

The favourite duck of the poacher was probably the Mallard, they were most common and quite meaty. The poacher would have caught duck primarily to eat but would have made the most of its feathers too. If he was lucky enough to capture an Eider Duck he would most certainly appreciated the down it provided. It is unlikely he would have caught enough duck to trade; men employed as wildfowlers would have had this job and used the Duck Decoys when possible.

Pheasant

Pheasant is typically considered the choice of the Aristocracy. There is an age-old question - How long should you hang a pheasant before you cook it? A poacher's answer: Pluck, gut and put it in the oven straight away - why? The family is hungry!

British poultry farmers can be applauded as they they can rear a day old chicken to an oven ready bird in 42 days (seven harvests in 52 weeks) but unfortunately they are without much taste. This has opened up the market for *'cook in sauces'* for chicken, which is worth up to £2 million pounds a year. A colourful cock pheasant with a white ring around its neck is at least 18 months old and full of flavour without a *'cook-in sauce'*.

Plate 141 - Pheasants: Cock and Two Hens
A.W. Seaby

Other pheasant lore: If you burn their feathers they stink! Plus you give away the fact you have eaten evidence of a crime! More sensible suggestions to avoid capture are *'Push 'em down the 'privy'* at the bottom of the garden' or to put them in a trench where you are growing a row of potatoes. Make a nest of the feathers, place seed potatoes in the centre, cover with feathers and then the soil. You will get blemish free potatoes and rotting down the feathers will release nitrogen for a fertile crop.

The poacher would not only collect his quarry to eat but also to exchange for much needed essentials. Coal was a valuable commodity and if a poacher was lucky, his cottage would have a cooking range. This range would provide warmth and heat for the dwelling as well as for cooking and baking. An old North Lincolnshire discipline was to first spend your hard earned money on coal to survive the Winter. Even then, the money earned may not have stretched far enough for the supplu enough coal for the entire Winter and thus income needed to be supplemented.

In the 1930's, coal was approximately £12/ton and when the county started growing sugar beet, a ton of it cost the same (now, coal is circa £300/ton and sugar beet £22/ton). Extra money raised from poaching would be greatly needed and appreciated. The exchange rate for a brace of pheasants was 2 shillings and sixpence (half a crown). An old hare was 5 shillings (one full crown) though often these things were exchanged for a bag of coal or to pay doctor's or butcher's bills.

Often, the landlord of the local hostelry kept a .410 shotgun behind the bar and let the poacher use it in exchange for a pheasant. Some landlords also kept a Lurcher dog, or pair of Longdogs, for the poacher to use, this would mean if he did get caught, he would have less incriminating evidence. With the network of small rural railway stations, the poacher could send his game to Lincoln, Boston and Nottingham or further afield to London.

Pigeon

The poacher would probably not have been accused of poaching if found with pigeons as they were plentiful and often ate the food left out for game. However, if he was caught at the wrong time of day the Game Laws would favour landowners so he still had to be careful.

Plate 90 - Ring Dove Courting
A.W. Seaby

The poacher had an extra trick up his sleeve when finding a pigeon nest. If there was more than one chick, he would kill all but one of the young, and tie a piece of string around the remaining bird and attach it to a branch so it could not fly away once it reached flying age. This ensured the parents of the remaining squab would continue to feed it, ensuring it would get plump, a delicious luxury for the poacher's family!

Fish

There was little in the way of fish breeding in Lincolnshire, one or two trout streams, but certainly no salmon. Lincolnshire does not have much in the way of fast-flowing rivers, it tends to be slow-moving and semi-stagnant, so much of the 'water-game' was 'fair game'.

Poachers would have known where trout and pike liked to rest and swim, they may have tickled them out of the water (or netted them). One creature which was in plentiful supply was eel, not a food landowners were particularly interested in eating. Despite this, if a poacher was found trespassing they may well have been charged.

Eggs

If the poacher's family was lucky, they may have kept chickens. Hen's eggs would have been much welcomed in hard times. However, not all poacher families were so fortunate. During the breeding season of game, the poacher would have looked carefully for an abandoned nest to see if any eggs were available.

Plate 194 - Eggs:
H. Grönveld

1 - Partridge
2 - Redlegged Partridge
3 - Red-grouse
4 - Ptarmigan
5 - Pheasant
6 - Quail
7 - Capercaillie
8 - Black-grouse

He would have been respectful of nesting game though, and more wary, as these hens would continue the longevity of a covey or flock. To interfere would ultimately cause hunger in following years and make the gamekeeper more certain to be on the lookout.

Lincolnshire Spinach

In addition to the meat the poacher would catch, wherever possible the family would grow what they could in their gardens or yards. This included a plant called 'Lincolnshire Spinach', sometimes called Good King Henry, Markery or Poor Man's Asparagus. It is a species of goosefoot native to central and southern Europe. The plant can grow between 40-80cm high and has leaves of 5-10cm with a slightly waxy, succulent texture. The flowers are small, green with 5 sepals and are produced on a tall spike. The seeds are a reddish-green and 2-3mm in diameter. According to Stanley Scaman of Theddlethorpe, it is the only vegetable that is completely pest-free, even the slugs wont eat it and yet the Poachers family did!

*On the table there lay set
A feast for the intrepid man.*

6
The Poacher's Remorse

In 1723, The Black Act authorised the death penalty for more than 50 poaching offences. It remained law for nearly a century and after it was repealed, poachers were transported instead. In the same period, to reinforce the laws and deter poachers, landowners used '*man-traps*', '*spring guns*' and trip-wire operated '*dog spears*' on their land.

Man-traps were made illegal in 1826 but a law in 1830 enabled landowners to apply for a licence to use them. Gertrude Jekyll, of Surrey, wrote in 1904, that she had observed notices warning of such devices on the outside of plantations, despite the fact they were finally banned in 1861.

This example of a man-trap is from the collection of the late Peter Moore of Moor Farm, Bloxham.

Despite all these deterrents and penalties, a poacher's fare was likely to be the only way in which their families (along with other poor families who were lucky enough to know a poacher) were able to survive. Therefore, they may have felt they had no option other than to partake in this profession. Would they have felt remorse for feeding their starving families? Probably not; however, being caught may have caused many a regret!

How many Lincolnshire Poachers were there?

Whilst the exact figure can never really be confirmed we can make some assumptions to predict how many Lincolnshire Poachers there may have been. The county has about 300 villages and supposing there was one poacher per village there would be about 300 at any given time. In a county as large as Lincolnshire, there was room for them all. In larger townships however, there might have been as many as half a dozen.

We can confirm the numbers of Lincolnshire Poachers caught by using the records that are held in Lincoln Castle (previously a Court and Prison). If a poacher was caught their odds were not favourable as these records show.

The records in Lincoln Castle provide a rare list showing all poachers caught, their punishment and where they ended up. It is thought that one third of all English men in jail at this time were there for breaking Game Laws.

Many offenders were sentenced to hard labour, penal servitude (within the UK), imprisonment or transportation to the British colonies. Transportation was considered the worst punishment, as families knew they were unlikely to see their loved ones again; many people died on the crossings alone.

Lincoln Castle Records

The records from Lincoln Castle have been extracted from an extensive database created by Chris and Sheila Collins. When they volunteered at the Castle they developed a passion for ensuring information was preserved. They found a number of records thought to be previously unknown to the curators of the castle.

They poured painstakingly over many documents to collate the database, which now holds over 14,500 entries of prisoners who were held at the Castle. In this book, we have only published the records of those tried for poaching and offences related to poaching. In the earlier records, some offences were recorded as *'Poaching Rabbits'* or *'Poaching Conies'*. There are ten entries recorded as *'Poaching and Assault'* and one entry as *'Poaching with Gun'*. There are two other notable entries: William Radsdale, who was sentenced to death and then transported for ten years, plus the infamous William Clarke, who was accused of murder and executed on 26th March 1877. He is mentioned further in this chapter. All named prisoners are recorded in red in the table.

During the time the records were created, there was little consistency as to what was written down and where the entries recorded. The information was collated using many sources, including: Crown Calendars, Crown Sentences, Assize Calendars, Surgeons Records, Chaplain's Journals, Calendar of Prisoners, Calendar of Sentences, Clerks Papers, Felons Registers, Gaoler Journals, Governor Journals and Prisoner Weight Records.

The Assize Calendars were documents published several times a year, prior to trial. The Calendar of Prisoners were documents published after sentencing had been made.

The Lincolnshire Poacher

The Calendar of Prisoners were intended for public viewing, very much in the style as you see in films made of the era: a proclamation being nailed into a post or wall.

The records used to find the information in the tables are very delicate and some in disrepair making it very difficult or impossible to read all the detail provided at the original time. As much information has been provided as possible to the best possible accuracy. Many records were actually destroyed between 1800 and 1820 (the period of the Napoleonic Wars).

As you can imagine, the number of people responsible for recording information would have been vast, plus each type of record book would have required different information. In addition to this, each person would have had their own idiosyncrasies, interests and time constraints, adding or omitting detail as they saw fit. You will notice some entries have: the height or weight of a prisoner; age, abode and occupation; if the prisoner was married and had children; and various other anomalies while others have very little recorded at all. Some prisoners have been noted in more than one record (this may be why there are extra details for them).

You will note that in only a few cases, a religion was recorded for the prisoner. It was generally assumed that the prisoner would be Methodist or Church of England at this time. If the prisoner was Catholic, a separate service may have been provided for them if they so wished.

However, the date prisoners were first confined at the Castle was recorded for all prisoners. In some cases, such as George Moody, the day he was first confined at the prison is not actually known due to the condition of the records but he is recorded in the Assizes Calendar on 4th March 1854 so the 1st March 1854 has been entered.

The Poacher's Remorse

The Prison Doctor would have made his rounds every day, most likely in the morning. New prisoners would be examined and recorded in his journal. In addition to examining new detainees, he would also have attended any prisoner who was reported to be sick and an extra entry for them would have been made in his Surgeons Record, demonstrated in the entry for Charles Cree.

A few prisoners are mentioned more than once, such as John Smith (whether this was his real name, I'll let you decide). It is thought to be the same person as his age and confinement dates correspond accurately.

When the original records were made, the entry makers are unlikely to have used any abbreviations at all, writing out all the details in careful, precise script. All abbreviations used in the tables are modern and used to aid consistency.

Abbrev	Meaning	Abbrev	Meaning
AC	Assize Calendar	#c	number of children
CC	Crown Calendar	ba	baker
CJ	Chaplains Journal	bm	boatman
CoP	Calendar of Prisoners	br	brickmaker
CoS	Calendar of Sentences	bu	butcher
CP	Clerks Papers	c	convict
CS	Crown Sentences	Ca	Catholic
FR	Felons Register	cs	chimney sweep
GaJ	Gaoler Journal	fa	farmer
GIB	Gibraltar	fc	filecutter
GoJ	Governors Journal	l	labourer
HC	House of Correction	m	months
HL	Hard Labour	p	poacher
M	Married	pc	previous convictions
NSW	New South Wales (Australia)	s	sawyer
PS	Penal Servitude	sh	shoemaker
PWR	Prisoners Weight Record	v	vagrant
SR	Surgeons Record	w	weeks
VDL	Van Diemans Land (Tasmania)	yr	year

The Lincolnshire Poacher

Name	Age	Job	Accomplices	Abode	Confined	Sentence	Comments
Ransley, Robert		c		Manton	05.03.1781	12m HL in HC	AC 28.07.1781 (Poaching Conies) (Rabbits are Property of R Brownlow)
Laming, William	35	fa		Born Croxby Lived North Kelsey	26.02.1791	Not Guilty 19.03.1791	FR Dark Skin, Black Beard, (Poaching Rabbits) (M) (5'8")
Tate, John	28	sh		Croxby Nr Caistor	28.01.1791	Acquitted 09.03.1791	FR Born Ashby Lived Brigg. (Poaching Rabbits) (M 2c) (5'8")
Longmate, Edward		l		Woodhall	24.12.1828	Acquitted 14.03.1829	CoS
Sharpe, William		l		Woodhall	24.12.1828	Acquitted 14.03.1829	CoS
Wooldridge, Thomas	45	l		Woodhall	24.12.1828	Transported for 7yrs	AC March 1829
Straw, John	36		Samuel Fiddler	Lincoln	02.12.1830	1yr HL 05.03.1831	SR 16.12.1830 Re Nocton Estate
Bee, William	20	br		Louth	29.01.1833	3m (For Trespass)	SR 08.02.1833 AC 09.03.1833
Cooper, James	21			Broughton	20.10.1834	Transported for 7 years	SR 20.10.1834 From Kirton H of C to NSW 1836
Hind, Thomas	21			Broughton	28.10.1834	Transported for 7 years	20.10.1834 Convicted at Kirton HC SR 28.10.1834 Moved To Woolwich Hulk 11.11.1834 To NSW 1836
Davy, Bennett	24			Bourne	09.01.1835	Transported for 7 Years	May have been aged 21 To VDL 1835 Convict from Falkingham HC
Fisher, Charles			Richard Johnson		21.11.1836	To Kirton HC 6m HL	SR 23.11.1836
Johnson, Richard			Charles Fisher		21.11.1836	To Kirton HC 6m HL	SR 23.11.1836
Jackson, John	31		Robert Kendall		08.01.1837	Bail 20.01.1837 Acquitted 03.1837	SR 08.01.1837
Stow, Thomas	40		William Thompson		08.01.1837	Bail 14.01 Acquitted 1837	SR 08.01.1837
Kendale or Kendall, Robert	28				08.03.1837	6m HL	SR 08.03.1837 To Kirton HC

The Poacher's Remorse

Name	Age	Job	Accomplices	Abode	Confined	Sentence	Comments
Thompson, William	28		Thomas Stow		08.03.1837	Bail 14.01.1837 Acquitted 1837	AC 1837
Semper, William		p		Bishop Norton Area	06.11.1839	To Kirton HC 08.11.1839	SR 06.11.1839 Shot wounds on body
Scott, Henry	23	l	Joseph Scott	Hacconby	18.10.1842	Transported for 10yrs	SR 18.10.1842 To VDL 1845 (Brother of Joseph)
Scott, Joseph	21		Henry Scott	Hacconby	18.10.1842	Transported for 10yrs	SR 18.10.1842 To GIB 1844 (Brother of Henry)
Flintham, Matthew					22.04.1844	To Kirton HC 24.04.1844	SR 22.04.1844 From Louth HC
Hollingsworth, Charles	34			Norton Disney	24.11.1844	14m HL	CC 18.12.1844 To Falkingham HC
Woodcock, John Gent	28			Norton Disney	24.11.1844	14m HL	SR 26.11.1844 AC 18.12.1844 To Falkingham HC
Brailsford, George	23		George Galland, Samuel Spencer	Norton Disney	19.01.1846	3m HL	AC 07.03.1846
Galland, George	39		George Brailsford, William Squires	Norton Disney	19.01.1846	3m HL	AC 07.03.1846
Squires, William	30		George Brailsford, William Squires	Norton Disney	19.01.1846	3m HL	AC 07.03.1846
Frudd, Thomas	40	bu	Samuel Kinder	Morton / Fillingham	12.11.1846	10m HL to Kirton HC	SR 06.03.1847
Kinder, Samuel	24		Thomas Frudd	Fillingham	12.11.1846	10m HL to Kirton HC	SR 06.03.1847
Rudd, Thomas	24			Hungerton	09.04.1847	9m 17.07.1847	SR 17.07.1847 From Falkingham HC
Beech, Robert	28		Thomas Beech, Robert Holland, William Drayton	Hemswell	02.03.1847	Acquitted	AC 03.03.1847 (Son of Thomas)
Beech, Thomas	55		Robert Beech, Robert Holland, William Drayton	Hemswell	02.03.1847	1yr HL	AC 03.03.1847 (Father of Robert)

49

The Lincolnshire Poacher

Name	Age	Job	Accomplices	Abode	Confined	Sentence	Comments
Drayton, William	28		Robert Beech, Thomas Beech, Robert Holland	Hemswell	09.03.1847	Acquitted	AC 03.03.1847
Gadow, Joseph					09.03.1847	Acquitted	AC 03.03 1847
Holland, Robert	23		Robert Beech, Thomas Beech, William Drayton	Hemswell	09.03.1847	Acquitted	AC 03.03.1847
Preston, Thomas	22			West Halton/ Caborne	13.12.1848	Transported for 7yrs	SR 03.01.1849 (Single Man) To Wakefield then W AUS 1851
Langton, David	31		George Thomas	Apley	17.12.1848	12m HL	SR 18.12.1848 To Kirton HC 05.03.1849
Thomas, George	28		David Langton	Apley	17.12.1848	12m HL	SR 18.12.1848 Discharged 13.01.1849
Smith, John	33		Thomas Clarke, James Vickers	Bishop Norton	20.01.1848	5m Kirton HC 04.03.48	SR 20.01.1848 To Kirton HC
Vickers, James	31		Thomas Clarke, John Smith	Bishop Norton	20.01.1848	5m Kirton HC	AC 04.03.1848
Spencer, Samuel					01.03.1848	To Falkingham HC	CJ
Clarke, Thomas	30		James Vickers, John Smith	Bishop Norton	04.03.1848	6m Kirton HC	AC 04.03.1848
Thompson, Matthew		l			26.05.1848	For re - hearing	CJ
Fowler, Thomas	27		Enoch Jordan, Charles Tindall		26.02.1849	3m HL	SR 27.02.1849 CC 06.03.1849
Jordan, Enoch	19	br		Eagle	26.02.1849	12m HL	SR 27.02.1849 CC 06.03.1849 To Kirton HC (Brother of John)
Tindall, Charles	21		Thomas Fowler, Enoch Jordan		26.02.1849	12m HL	SR 27.02.1849 CC 06.03.1849

The Poacher's Remorse

Name	Age	Job	Accomplices	Abode	Confined	Sentence	Comments
Locking, John			Tom Preston	West Lindsey Area	03.01.1849	2yrs HL	SR 03.01.1849 To Kirton HC 08.03.1849
Schofield, William	22				05.09.1849	Transported for 7yrs	From Louth Sessions Committed 06.09.49
York, George	26				05.09.1849	Transported for 7yrs	From Louth Sessions Committed 06.09.49 (alias Mathew Hawkins)
Higgins, Robert	22		John Robinson	Spilsby Area	01.02.1850	Tried 09.03.50 1yr HL	SR 13.03.1850 From and to Spilsby HC
Robinson, John	42			Bullington	11.01.1850	1yr To Kirton HC	
Fieldsend, George	49		Samuel Mobbs, John Smith	Redbourne Area	01.03.1850	8m HL Kirton HC 03.1850	SR 02.03.1850 From Kirton HC
Mobbs, Samuel	30		Martin Wilkinson, John Smith	Redbourne Area	01.03.1850	8m HL Kirton HC 15.0	SR 02.03.1850 From Kirton HC
Smith, John	37			Redbourne Area	01.03.1850	1yr HL to Kirton HC 15.0	SR 02.03.1850 From Kirton HC (Tried before for Poaching)
Wilkinson, Martin	37		George Fieldsend, Samuel Mobbs	Redbourne Area	01.03.1850	6m HL Tried 09.03.1850	CSs 09.03.50 From Kirton HC
Brown, Frederick	25		Samuel Mobbs, John Smith, Fieldsend, George	Redbourne Area	12.03.1850	6w HL Kirton HC 15.03.1850	CS 09.03.50 SR 13.03.1850
Radsdale, William	19			Greeton Area	16.08.1851	Death Commuted to Transportation for 10 yrs	SR 15.08.1851 To Wakefield HC 01.05.1852 (Shot Gamekeeper)
Tupling, George					04.03.1851	6m HL	CS 05.03.1851 SR 10.03.51 (Poaching with Gun)
Brown, Robert			Mark Holmes		20.12.1852	6m Spilsby HC	SR 21.12.1852 CC 26.02.1853
Holmes, Mark			Robert Brown		20.12.1852	6m Spilsby HC	SR 21.12.1852 CC 26.02.1853
Fielding, Abraham					08.05.1852	Awaiting Trial	SR 08.05.1852

The Lincolnshire Poacher

Name	Age	Job	Accomplices	Abode	Confined	Sentence	Comments
Lockwood, Richard					08.05.1852	Awaiting Trial	SR 08.05.1852
Watson, Thomas	19	I		Born Thurlby	14.04.1853	Transported 7yrs Tried Bourne 04.1853	AC 17.05.53 To Wakefield (Poaching and Assault) (Brown Hair, Hazel Eyes) (5'8")
Wilson, Thomas	38	I		Born Dunsby Nr Bourne	14.04.1853	Transported 7yrs Tried Bourne 04.1853	To Wakefield 17.05.53 (Poaching and Assault) (Brown Hair. Hazel eyes) (M 5c) (5'9")
Lowe, William					01.12.1853	Awaiting Trial	AC 04.03.1854
Moody, George					01.12.1853	Awaiting Trial	AC 04.03.1854
Mumby, Joseph					01.12.1853	Awaiting Trial	AC 04.03.1854
Smith, John				Bishop Norton Area	18.01.1855	To Kirton HC 20.01.1855	GJ 1855 Released to Police at 12 noon (10th time for Poaching)
Graham, John					01.10.1855	To Falkingham HC 10.12.1855	GoJ 1855
Bradshaw, Jonathan	40	I	James Horsewood	Haugham	24.12.1856	3m HL	SR 27.12.1858 To Louth HC 03.1859
Wilkinson, William	39	I		Louth Area	06.12.1857	4yrs Penal Servitude	SR 07.12.1857
Thompson, John					12.07.1857	On Remand Discharged 13.07	SR 13.07.1857
Broughton, Joseph	31	I		Louth Area	13.07.1857	On Remand Discharged 14.07.1857	SR 13.07.1857
Gilbert, Alice	29			Waddington	27.11.1857	Acquitted	CP (Wife of Oliver)
Graby, George	27	I	Thomas Wilkinson	Bishop Norton Area	21.12.1858	6m HL	CJ 14.03.59 To Kirton HC 14.07.59
Wilkinson, Thomas	35	I	George Graby	Kirton Area	21.12.1858	6m HL	SR 24.02.1859 To Kirton HC
Atkin, Robert	46	I		Haugham	24.12.1858	3m HL	SR 27.12.1858 To Louth HC 03.1859

The Poacher's Remorse

Name	Age	Job	Accomplices	Abode	Confined	Sentence	Comments
Gilbert, George	38	l	William Woolhouse	Bishop Norton Area	24.12.1858	6m HL	SR 27.12.1858 To Kirton HC 03.1859
Horsewood, James	26	l		Haugham	24.12.1858	3m HL	SR 27.12.1858 To Louth HC 03.1859
Woolhouse, William			Jonathan Bradshaw, George Gilbert		24.12.1858	On Remand	CJ SR 27.12.1858
Ross, James	24	l		Born Middlewit, Cheshire	07.07.1858	4yrs Penal servitude From Falkingham HC 28.06.1858	AC To Millbank 02.08.1858 (Poaching and Assault) (M 2c) (Ca) (5'11")
Yates, George	31	s, l		Born St Georges Stamford	07.07.1858	3yrs Tried Bourne 28.06.1858	SR 08.07.1858 To Millbank 02.08.58 (Poaching and Assault) (M 3c) (5'5")
Webster, Thomas					06.11.1858	On Remand	CJ
Wyles, John					17.09.1858	To Falkingham HC 18.09.58	CJ
Auckland, George			John Baker		26.04.1859	Remand To Falkingham HC	CJ 07.05.1859
Wallis, William	30	l			30.12.1859	6m HL	AC 12.03.1858 To Kirton HC
Newborn, Joseph	43	l	William Peacock	Burnham	05.07.1859	23m Kirton HC 01.08.1859	CoP 23.07.1859 (Poaching and Assault)
Peacock, William	43	l	John Newborn	Burnham	05.07.1859	15m Kirton HC 27.07.1859	SR 07.07.1859 CoP 23.07.1859 (Poaching and Assault)
Newborn, William					06.07.1859	To Kirton HC 29.07.1859	SR 07.07.1859
Graby, George	27		John Baker		14.07.1859	Remand To Kirton HC	CJ 16.07.1859
Brown, William	28			Kirton	28.07.1859	3m	SR 07.09.1859
Hand, Edward	45	l		Haugham	12.03.1859	5m HL Louth HC	CP
Lee, Jonathan		v	William Porter		19.11.1859	On Remand	CJ
Porter, William			Jonathan Lee		19.11.1859	On Remand	CJ

53

The Lincolnshire Poacher

Name	Age	Job	Accomplices	Abode	Confined	Sentence	Comments
Raithsby, Thomas	40	—			01.04.1860	On Remand	SR 02.04.1860
Graham, John	30	—			08.12.1860	12m HL	13.12.1860 To Folkingham HC
Smith, Aizy	36	cs			08.12.1860	4yrs PS	Removed To Wakefield Prison 17.01.1861 (Cell C19)
Holdbrook, Thomas	35	—		Born Bolingbroke	18.12.1860	4 yrs	SR 31.01.1861 To Wakefield 22.06.1861 (Cell B5)
Lester, Thomas	29	—			18.12.1860	12m HL	SR 18.12.1860 To Kirton HC 19.03.1861 (Cell B12)
Stevenson, George	49	—			18.12.1860	4yrs	SR 18.12.1860 To Wakefield 22.06.1861 (Cell B)
Swift, William		fc		Born Sheffield	19.12.1860	12m HL	SR 21.03.1861 To Kirton HC 19.03.1861 (M) (Cell B9)
Gilbert, George	36	—	John Graham		22.10.1860	18m HL Falkingham HC	CJ and CP
Baker, John	38	—		Nocton Area	07.05.1861	18m HL	SR 13.05.1861 To Falkingham HC 26.07.1861 (Syphilis)
Wilkinson, Thomas	38	b, c		Kirton Area	14.08.1862	12m HL	SR 14.08.1862 Kirton HC (Felon)
Cree, Charles	30	—	James Martin, Charles Cree	Scotton	18.10.1862	14yrs PS	CoP 09.12.1862 SR 18.12.1862 and 27.10.1862 (Poaching and Assault)
Hobson, Henry	32	bm		Scotton	18.10.1862	10yrs To Wakefield 02.03.1863	CoP 08.12.1862 SR 27.10.1862 (Poaching and Assault)
Rowbotham, William	28	bm	Charles Cree, Henry Hobson	Scotton	18.10.1862	15m Falkingham HC	CoP 09.12.1862 SR 27.10.1862 (Poaching and Assault)
Martin, James		bm		Scotton	27.10.1862	10yrs to Wakefield 02.03.63	CoP 09.12.1862 SR 27.10.1862 (Poaching and Assault)

The Poacher's Remorse

Name	Age	Job	Accomplices	Abode	Confined	Sentence	Comments
Gilbert, George			John Smith, Thomas Williamson		14.04.1863	To Kirton HC 24.03.1863	CJ
Thompson, John					08.12.1863	To Louth HC 18.03.1864	SR 09.12.1863
Smith, John	49	l	George Gilbert, Thomas Williamson	Kirton Area	14.03.1863	12m To Kirton HC 24.03	SR 16.03.1863 To Kirton HC
Williamson, Thomas			John Smith		14.03.1863	To Kirton HC 24.03.1863	CJ
Hind, John					10.12.1864	Awaiting Trial	CJ
Ealand, Thomas	36	l		Born and lived Horncastle	16.01.1864	3yr Tried Spilsby 20.02.1864	SR 19.01.1864 To Wakefield 20.02.64 (9 pc) (Son of Richard) (Brown Hair, Blue Eyes) (5'6")
Blanchard, Henry			Jesse Boucher, William Marshall		05.11.1864	To Spilsby HC 22.03.1865	SR 05.11.1864
Boucher, Jesse			Henry Blanchard, William Marshall		05.11.1864	To Spilsby HC 22.03.1865	SR 05.11.1864
Marshall, William			Henry Blanchard, Jesse Boucher		05.11.1864	To Spilsby HC 22.03.1865	SR 05.11.1864
Coulbeck, George			Geo Stokes		27.01.1865	Awaiting Trial	CJ
Stokes, George			Geo Coulbeck		27.01.1865	Discharged 17.03.1865	SR 28.01.1865
Jackson, Shiner					10.10.1866	Awaiting Trial	SR 10.10.1866 To Kirton HC 08.12.1866 (Sick) (10st 0lb)
Bell, William			John Gilbert		07.03.1866	To Kirton HC 22.03.1866	SR 08.03.1866 CJ (12st 8lb)
Gilbert, John	33	ba		Corringham	07.03.1866	To Wakefield 12.05.1866	CJ and PWR (10st 2lb)
Wells, William Humphrey	30			Corringham	07.03.1866	To Kirton HC 22.03.1866	SR 08.03.1866 CJ (11st 11lb)
Humphrey, William			William Bell		08.03.1866	Awaiting Trial	CJ

The Lincolnshire Poacher

Name	Age	Job	Accomplices	Abode	Confined	Sentence	Comments
Symonds, Robert					01.10.1866	Guilty	To Millbank 16.01.1867
Franklin, Charles					09.10.1866	Guilty	SR 10.10.1866 To Millbank 15.02.1867 (12st 2lb)
Gillatt, John					10.10.1866	Awaiting Trial	SR 10.10.1866 To Kirton HC 08.12.1866 (11st 0lb)
Marshall, William					10.10.1866	Awaiting Trial	SR 10.10.1866 To Kirton HC 08.12.1866 (11st 6lb)
Graham, Jonathan					28.11.1868	To Falkingham HC 19.12.68	CJ and PWR (11st 2lb)
Teaster, Jonathan					28.11.1868	To Falkingham HC 18.12.68	CJ and PWR (9st 9lb)
Ashton, Thomas					22.07.1869	Acquitted 24.07.1869	CJ and PWR (12st 5lb)
Hand, Edward	57	1		South Carlton Area	09.01.1871	Removed 17.03.1871	PWR 17.03.1871 To Kirton HC (10st 11lb)
Franklin, Charles					23.07.1873	Discharged 24.03.1873	PWR (Ca) (13st 8lb)
Newborn, John					18.03.1873	Awaiting Trial	CJ
Sewell, Joseph					24.11.1874	To Spilsby HC 24.03.75	SR 25.01.1875 CJ 03.75 (9st 11lb)
Hutson, Henry					13.03.1875	To Spilsby HC 24.03.75	CJ
Clarke, William	44				20.02.1877	Executed 26.03.1877	PWR Executed 9 am (Murder) (alias Slenderman) (13st 13lb)
Mawley, Thomas			Thomas Rose	Nottingham Gaol	20.01.1878	Awaiting Trial	CJ
Rose, Thomas			George Woodcock	Nottingham Gaol	20.01.1878	Guilty	CJ To Nottingham Gaol 25.01.78
Tomlinson, Richard			Thomas Rose	Nottingham Gaol	20.01.1878	Guilty	CJ To Nottingham Gaol 25.01.78
Woodcock, George			Thomas Rose	Nottingham Gaol	20.01.1878	Guilty	CJ To Nottingham Gaol 25.01.78

The Poacher's Remorse

There were some unusual places where prisoners were sent. Many who were convicted were imprisoned locally but others, if not transported, were sent further away in the UK. For instance Thomas Hind, was sentenced for transportation for seven years. Prior to transportation he was sent to Woolwich Hulk.

A *'hulk'* was a decommissioned ship the authorities used as floating prisons. Hulks were ships that were afloat, but incapable of going to sea. They should not be mistaken for *'convict ships'*, which were seaworthy vessels and transported convicted felons to their place of banishment.

The poachers who suffered the most from being transported, were those who were sent to Virginia to work on the tobacco and cotton fields. They were indentured to the large plantations and literally worked to death. Plantation owners believed there was no need to look after them as well as they looked after their black slaves, thus their life expectancy was short.

There are stories of Lincolnshire Lads who were deported. Naturally, as Lincolnshire lads, they took a few tricks with them and one of them was how to make genuine Lincolnshire sausage. This was so good that the Americans copied the recipe and called it *'Virginia Sausage'*.

Virginia Sausage	Lincolnshire Sausage
1 lb ground pork	700g pork shoulder or belly
3 tsp dried sage	10g fresh sage (chopped)
1½ tsp salt	150g dry wheat roll or bread
¾ tsp ground black pepper	150g water
¼ tsp dried marjoram	18g salt
¾ tbsp brown sugar	4g white pepper
1 pinch ground cloves	

Shown above are the similarities between the two recipes. The Lincolnshire recipe has been passed down to me from my mother. She didn't use a weighing machine or scales; she put down a special cloth, wiped the sides clean and put all the ingredients in - a spoonful of this and that, just using her *'Lincolnshire instincts'*.

Slenderman

There is a famous and notorious poacher called William Clarke (alias *'Slenderman'*). Technically he isn't a *'Lincolnshire Poacher'* as he hailed from Nottingham. William Clarke was part of a gang of poachers caught at Norton Disney; at this incident a gamekeeper was shot and later died.

However, Clarke was not apprehended until a later time. Eventually, he was confined at the Castle on 20th February 1877. He was tried for the murder of the shot gamekeeper but there is speculation as to whether he was actually the poacher who fired the shot. It is also thought that there was a delay in the gamekeeper receiving medical treatment, which may have contributed to his demise.

Incidentally, he was the last person to be executed at the Castle. Perhaps the discrepancies of the case caused them to rethink this penalty! Therefore, despite being from Nottinghamshire, he has a very compelling reason to be mentioned in this book.

The Poacher's Remorse

It is also reported that it is his dog which is stuffed and has been placed in a case within the castle. Over the years, reports have been made of a dog apparition at the Castle and the Strugglers Inn (where Clarke used to frequent). The Strugglers Inn is still a public house today. It is situated on Westgate, outside the Northern tip of the Castle walls. Former landlords have reported whining and scratching at the doors of the Inn late at night as if the dog is still searching for his master.

The Slenderman has a blue English Heritage plaque dedicated to him on a wall at the castle. The plaque also has a section of the song 'The Lincolnshire Poacher'. A popular song at the time and which still has a popular following today. I have dedicated a whole chapter to the song, see Chapter 10 - The Lincolnshire Poacher Song.

Lincolnshire's A and B Teams

I once came across a lady who was researching her family history, and believed her relative was a poacher. She was concerned that they weren't in the records. I said, '*Well, those on the list were the ones which were caught, Lincolnshire's B Team. But if he wasn't caught, he was Lincolnshire's A team!*' She thought it was a good explanation.

POLICE

An Understanding Lincolnshire Bobby

Bill Anderson was a local bobby in Horncastle and he lived in one of the nearby villages. One morning, his phone started ringing, several local farmers and reported lots of poaching overnight. Bill said he already knew. '*How*?' asked the farmers. Bill replied they had left him a brace of pheasants hanging from his back door as a common courtesy.

Police Poaching from the Poachers

There is a story (before modern refrigeration) that one police station in the South Lincolnshire Fens caught so many poachers with full bags of freshly killed pheasants and they didn't want the game to go to waste. The pheasants from this region were hardier, faster and plumper than normal wild pheasants and made really good eating. So, they took the pheasant home for their wives to cook. It is reported they ate so many over the shooting season that the four officers all came down with gout (a very painful and debilitating condition caused by too much rich food) and so were not much use in catching poachers until they healed. This was the poacher's ultimate revenge!

Modern Policing - Operation Galileo

Operation Galileo is a National Police Campaign was re-launched in Lincolnshire in 2018 and aims to work alongside the public and other bodies, such as the NFU. It focuses on all aspects of rural crime across the county, not only on poaching or hare coursing. The effort by all parties is beginning to pay off and a reduction of incidents is starting to be seen.

Lincolnshire Police and Crime Commissioner Marc Jones said: *"I am delighted the investments I have made in cutting edge technology and equipment specifically designed for use in rural areas is making a difference. Hare coursers do not just have a negative impact on farming communities. The gangs that peddle in this cruel pursuit are responsible for other crimes across our rural communities and our road network."*

It is crucial to point out here that a true Lincolnshire Poacher did not capture hare or other game for sport as modern hare coursers do. The modern coursers have little regard for the countryside and nature's balance. The Lincolnshire Poacher would have had a profound respect for the countryside and only taken what was needed to survive.

The Lincolnshire Poacher

*Success to every gentleman
Who lives in Lincolnshire.*

7
The Poacher Stories

Here are a collection of unusual anecdotes and stories I have collected. Some have been retold to me by others, usually proffered to me after my talks, knowing that would enjoy hearing them. The poacher was such an integral part of the community the locals often knew him by name.

The Wall Street Journal

How many Lincolnshire people have had an article written about them in the Wall Street Journal? The Lincolnshire Poacher managed it. It appeared in the edition published on 18th October 1991 and started as thus: *'Very dark plots are a foot in England, as grouse grow fat - it's Gamekeeper vs. Poacher in an Old Feudal Rite.'* It continues, telling the story of Alan Count, the gamekeeper in the Nocton area of Lincolnshire, and the poacher whose *'nom de guerre'* was said to be Charles Peace. Each personality states his duty or right to the game on the ancestral estates of the aristocracy.

It is reported that Alan Count, a keeper for 35 of his 53 years, believed he and the poacher to be evenly matched, *"The poacher knows most of my tricks and I know most of his. We're heads and tails of the same coin."*

The article continues to emphasizes that the role of gamekeeper is not romantic as portrayed in D. H. Lawrence's *Lady Chatterley's Lover*, but it did offer an *'escape from class-ridden rural life'*. Mr Count felt although the land belonged to the rich he believed it was also his, *"If you're a keeper, the land is your beat. It belongs to you."* He felt it was his to protect from the many pests that featured upon it, including the poacher.

The poacher, who once dreamed of game keeping, but was unable to secure a post, states the opposite stance, *"I loathe aristocracy; game was put on this earth for every man. I'm just part of the natural balance."*

The article renders a believable account of the guerrilla warfare waged from both sides synonymous with poaching stories across Lincolnshire throughout the ages.

Charles Peace

On speaking to Charles Peace, he revealed a little more about this interview. He met the journalist in a dark corner of a village hall to tell him his side of the story. After the tale, Charles showed him the skill achievable with a catapult. The journalist placed a tin 25 yards away from Charles who hit it with no problem at all in the dark. The journalist took that tin back with him to America to show his colleagues what this British man could do!

Charles only poached as a young lad and teenager out of necessity. He came from a large family with eight children. He says, "*Poaching was a rite of passage and we put necessary meat on the table.*" Charles recalls he and his brothers (who all learned how to use a sling shot or catapult from a very early age), would head out early in the evning and catch a few birds, which went into the family food chain. Nothing was caught for commercial value.

The best time for poaching was in dark, inclement weather with low cloud cover. They would take note of which way the wind blew so they knew which side of the trees or hedges the birds would be roosting. They went out early and got home '*well before the gamekeeper had finished his tea*'. They did not want to be out at the same time as him.

He revealed he had on one occasion been surrounded by keepers. It was essential he was not seen or heard. He lay down low and kept very still. The keepers were so close he could have reached out and touched them. Fortunately for him, they did not even know he was there!

Charles took his alias from an 18th century villain who was never caught. Charley, a derivative of Charles is an old Lincolnshire term for a fox, well known as a wily creature.

As mentioned in the Wall Street Journal, Charles loathed the aristocracy. It was for this reason his main quarry was pheasant - a status symbol for the bluebloods. He remembers seeing his father doff his hat to the local squire and vowed he would never do that. Poaching was his way to claim what he felt entitled to from the land.

Charles says he only poached until he was about 20 years old, and reiterates it was only for necessity. He is not proud of his poaching history. Since this time, he has switched sides and has worked as a gamekeeper ever since.

He has caught poachers himself, but these poachers are of a different ilk to his former self. The modern poachers arrive in the county in great groups for commercial reasons. They have no respect for their quarry. They just kill it, sling it down and leave the game in the field, "*These modern types give the country way of life a bad name.*" Charles believes, "*A true poacher respects his quarry before and after he catches it.*"

Poacher's Ghosts

On the outskirts of Billinghay is a place called '*The Spirits*', local people believed it was haunted. Strange glows were seen in the willow woods at night. Now, it

| THE WHYCHE | SPRITE LANE |

is an old people's bungalow complex but the names of the roads around the area reflect the ghostly tales, '*The Whyche*' and '*Sprite Lane*'.

Back in the past, the poacher took advantage of rumour and stories, spreading tales of ghostly goings on and heightened the mystery of the fens to keep other folk away so they had the land all for themselves.

The stories include the '*Ghost Bird*' or '*Phosphorous Owl*'. If you saw this skinny bird coming towards you it would give you a fright. The poacher, however, knew that they were just owls who sheltered in ancient willow trees. As willows age they twist and crack and rot; at the centre of the trunks grow mushy old wood that gave home to hundreds of glow-worms (in fact a beetle that lives and thrives in this strange environment).

These '*glow-worms*' gave off a phosphorous element and then the phosphorous rubs onto the owl's feathers making them appear to glow too. It is also a phenomenon known in Norfolk as '*Eleuminated* Owls*'.
*Purposely misspelt to depict old dialect.

Jack O'Lantern, Will O' The Wisp

Another natural phenomena of the fens is rotting organic matter in the soil. It produces a self-igniting methane gas that sometimes stays in one place or a slight breeze can carry it along. The explanation for this phenomenon is called bioluminescence caused by the oxidation of phosphorous and methane. If you are unaware of this, it can seem otherworldly and can be quite scary.

Again the poacher would have known of this natural fenland oddity but would have definitely exploited the Victorian and pre-Victorian superstitions to his own gain.

Several years ago a female professor from one of our universities had a letter in *Farmers Weekly* on whether anyone had seen this happen in recent years to which she drew a blank. This is likely because we have used up all the organic matter (humas) in the fens through modern farming and drainage.

Bishop's View

The Bishop of Lincoln (circa 1840-1860) was very concerned for the reputation of Lincolnshire because of the Poachers' infamy and decided he ought to do something about it.

So, one Winter's morning he decided to walk from Lincoln to Five Mile House along the River Witham to meet Malachi Jerborams, a known poacher, at his cottage there. It was a long walk for the Bishop and when he got there, the poacher was in and his wife was cooking a welcoming pot of stew. The poacher welcomed the Bishop, who willingly took up the invitation to have a meal with them, he had an appetite and a love for good food, and *'Boy, did that stew smell good!'*

The stew contained: poached rabbit, potatoes, carrots, leeks, onions, lentils, peas, spices and herbs. The poacher's wife served them out and the Bishop grabbed his spoon and was just starting to eat, when the poacher stopped and said, *'Bishop, I will just give thanks before we start.'* and said these words (originally attributed to Jonathan Swift):

> *"For rabbits young and rabbits old*
> *For rabbits hot and rabbits cold*
> *For rabbits tender and rabbits tough*
> *We thank you, Lord, we have enough!"*

Did the Bishop actually realise the stew contained poached meat? We'll never know - only God knows!

The Long Sighted Poacher

The long-sighted poacher would often carry a pair of what he'd call field glasses (binoculars) across the fields, but these were expensive and hard to get hold of, so he had to rely on natural eyesight. Fortunately, even though the poacher diet was fairly basic, it consisted of foods that contain a lot of Lutein and Zeaxantin, substances found naturally in nettles, buckwheat, and other foods in a typical poacher diet. Foods that contain these carotenoids help to accumulate the same substance in the retina, thus improving eyesight.

It is thought that the people with the best sight in the world are the Indigenous Australians (previously called Australian Aborigines) as their traditional diet is rich in these substances too. During the World Wars, it is recorded that the Border Patrol crews would include a couple of native Aborigines to help find and stop illegal immigrants, as they could see boats on the horizon with their extraordinary eyesight before the officers with binoculars could see it.

The poacher also believed if you had a gold ring in each ear, it improved *'long sight'*. He got this idea from the gypsies. Occasionally, in the drainage of the fens, a skeleton has been found with a gold ring in each side of the skull. The explanation for this is; a poacher, caught by the local gamekeeper and his gang, was killed and disposed of in the boggy morass of the fens.

If the poacher was to collect game today and needed to protect his eyesight, he would probably buy these supplements of Lutein and Zeaxantin from health foods shops rather than relying on gold earrings or eating Lincolnshire Spinach!

Poacher to the Rescue

In the 1940s, my Uncle George was in Boston Livestock Market and he saw this event take place. On market day, Boston was full of people: buyers, sellers, onlookers, and livestock: cattle, sheep, pigs and poultry all to be auctioned off - it was all hustle and bustle. A fine looking horse started rearing up and causing a commotion, it then rolled to the ground and laid still. Some shouted, *'It's got colic,'* another *'It's dying and should be put out of its misery'*, but no one knew what to do.

A local gypsy, well-known as a poacher, pushed through the crowd to take a look at the horse. He asked if anybody had an empty pop bottle. He filled the bottle three quarters full from a drinking trough and reached into his pocket. He pulled out a 12 bore cartridge, opened the end, threw out the lead pellets and wads, and poured the black powder into the bottle. He put his thumb on top and gave it a good shake. Getting someone to help him to hold the horse's head up, poured the concoction down his throat - gave it a drench of the mixture.

Within 10 minutes, the horse everybody thought was dead or dying, opened its eyes, twitched its ears and moved its legs. In another 10 minutes, it was on its knees and after a further 10 minutes, was on its feet, looking a picture of health. What was the secret of this recovery? Black powder contains, charcoal, saltpetre and sulphur. Did one of these ingredients, or was it them all together, which produced the miracle cure?

POACHERS IN WAR TIME

Lincolnshire Poacher, George Cross

In the dark days of World War Two, when scores of airfields were being built in Lincolnshire, a poacher was looking after his pheasants in Fulsby Wood behind Toft Hill Farm (on the A153), when he realised that the plane flying over his head was not making the sound he was familiar with and it seemed erratic in its movements.

As he was in the wood and it was fairly dark, he could not see it, then, all of a sudden he heard it accelerate at top speed. He thought that was unusual but continued with his activities. Then, within a few yards, a parachutist came gently through the trees landing close by. Not knowing what to do, he hid behind a low bush, thinking an unexpected visitor had rumbled him.

Looking closely, he realised the man was in a German uniform and was starting to undress to reveal civilian clothes underneath. He pulled down the parachute and wrapped his uniform and helmet in it. The poacher watched as the man went to a nearby dyke and shoved the bundle up the culvert to hide it. In a quandary, the poacher realised the man was a hated enemy German soldier sent to spy on either Coningsby or Woodhall Spa airfield. A quick decision had to be made.

Knowing the German soldier was likely to be armed with a 7mm Luger (automatic weapon with an 8 shot magazine) designed to kill a man but had to be cocked with two hands and made an audible click, the poacher used his single barrelled .410 designed for killing pheasants but had the capability to be cocked silently with one hand, perfect for this unexpected skirmish. The outcome: Germany nil – England one!

What happened to the body? Was it: buried in the wood? Fed to the pigs to destroy the evidence? Buried under a runway to rattle his bones every time a British plane took off? The poacher let the authorities know and there was a complete blackout and lockdown on this event.

Incidentally, Prime Minister Winston Churchill did not like the British people knowing about German spies landing on British soil, as it was bad for moral. So any extra morale-boosting stories he could spread he did.

Years later, the farmer at Toft Hill got fed up with the water not draining away, he decided to pull up the old bridge and put in a bigger culvert pipe. To his surprise, he found an old German helmet, buttons and belt buckle wrapped up in a rotting parachute canvas and cord. The Luger was never found. Maybe the poacher took it home as a war trophy. As all the players in this episode are long gone, we will probably never get to the bottom of it. Perhaps, the Lincolnshire Poacher deserves a posthumous award for bravery by a civilian in conflict: Lincolnshire Poacher G.C.

The late Dennis Scarborough, who worked on Toft Hill Farm as a young lad, told this event to me. He drove a tractor and when he drove at night, was not allowed to use lights and had to rely on moonlight and the cherry red glow of the manifold. Dennis later went on to be a brilliant self-taught diesel fitter to local farmer's tractors.

The Best Gamekeepers

There is an old proverb, *'the best gamekeepers are reformed poachers'*, as they know all the tricks of the trade. During both World Wars when country people were called up to serve their country, the poachers and game keepers were always allocated to sniper sections, as they were familiar with 'hide and seek' strategies and were naturally great stalkers and shots. Not just good shots with a shotgun but with rifles of which some of them were given .25 Rook rifles.

POW Camp

One of Lincolnshire's POW camps, housed both German and Italian prisoners. The prisoners were put to work on the local farms. In general, these POWs enjoyed working on the farms because many of them were countrymen, farmers or farm workers in peacetime. While working on the farms, they always got a good meal at dinnertime.

They were lightly guarded and sometimes escaped, just to go poaching. If caught, they went back usually with the poached pheasants or a brace of rabbits, but they came unstuck the time when they stole some sheep.

A group of Italian POWs snuck off for a few hours to rustle some sheep. They realised the authorities were looking for them, and the penalty for this crime would have invariably been greater than for a few pheasants. So, they threw the carcasses down the well on the local farm.

Original Survivalist

The Lincolnshire Poacher was used to carrying out his trade *'behind enemy lines'*. The foe in peacetime was the gamekeepers and landowners whose game he was after. He was used to being shot at and was a master of evasion techniques; crawling along dyke bottoms and hedgerow sides on hands and knees over frozen ground, to get a 'pot shot' in sleet and snow.

Statistics of WW1 show approximately 64% of gamekeepers and poachers survived, as they were used to guerrilla fighting. Whereas, only 25% of the aristocracy returned; they were accustomed to the pheasant being driven to them and shooting at their leisure.

Callsigns

It is believed that one of the Russian Deep State callsigns was the tune of the Lincolnshire Poacher played continuously 24 hours a day seven days a week to black out whatever message they were sending. The callsign number stations are mentioned more in Chapter 10 - The Lincolnshire Poacher Song.

If you put this callsign into a search engine, it shows exactly where it is in Russia but nobody has fathomed out exactly what they are doing. The place indicated has the same role as our Government Communications Headquarters (GCHQ). One of GCHQ's offshoots is RAF Digby, which is situated in prime Lincolnshire territory.

Timberland Poacher

As a young'un, I lived in Waterside and our local poacher was called John Dowse. He lived in Timberland and was well known for having a hard-hitting shotgun, a 12 bore, single barrel, 32" long full choke. Once, he was caught shooting a cock pheasant as the local landowner, C. L. Bembridge, drove past. They were on first name terms.

It was the first week in February and the shooting season was over and it was now illegal to shoot game. Mr Bembridge saw John Dowse shoot the bird and shouted across to him, *"John, you're doing two things wrong: first, that is my pheasant and second, it is out of season!"*

John, holding up the bird, said, "*First, it's my pheasant now and when I get home my wife will cook it and a sprinkling of salt and pepper will bring it into season!*"

Sheffield Visitors

There was talk of some enterprising Sheffield lads who worked shifts in the steel factories coming into Lincolnshire on a motorbike and sidecar and poaching down country lanes. The rider with the headlamp would spot the pheasants and rabbits and the passenger would shoot with a .410 rifle.

The killed game was swiftly picked up and put in the footwell and then they accelerated away. The village bobbies on their pushbikes did not stand a chance of catching them. When the local poaching fraternity realised what was happening they sorted the lads out, who found it was a long walk back to Sheffield.

Osmond's White Oils Horse Liniment

Osmond's White Oils horse liniment or embrocation was found in most farmhouse medicine cupboards. It was used as the '*go to remedy*' not just for livestock but for humans as well. The farmworkers suffered from painful back problems from carrying 16-18 cwt. of wheat beans and peas from the threshing machines to the upstairs of the granaries.

It was used for sprains, pulled muscles, twisted ankles, housemaids knee and tennis elbow - in fact as a general cure for all. I remember my mum putting it on my shoulder and it stung so much that I forgot what I was suffering from!

Local village football teams used it to put on players legs on bitter Winter days to protect them from the cold and, as they were often grudge matches, from injury too.

Yet the poacher's had another interest in the liniment, it contained camphor, which rabbits hate. Using rags drenched in it they used to shove them down the hole to keep the rabbits in if they were ferreting or to keep the rabbits out of they were using dogs or guns.

A famous Lincolnshire Poacher called Mackenzie 'Kenzie' Thorpe of Long Sutton (more on Kenzie below) used a lot of the liniment. It was said that you could smell him from 15 yards away. He used a lot on his ganzie to help with relief from his ailments of rheumatism and arthritis, which he suffered badly from in his later years.

Poaching was a cold, wet occupation in the winter months, so the poacher regularly got these complaints; Osmond's was the only way he could get some relief.

Kenzie Thorpe

Kenzire Thorpe is possibly the most well-known (or notorious) Lincolnshire Poacher. He has been extensively written about by subject masters such as John Humphries in his book, *'Poacher's Tales'* and in Derek Mills', *'The Lincolnshire Poachers'*, so I was reluctant to include him in my book.

However, Derek Mills actually states, *'In any book on poaching in Lincolnshire Kenzie certainly deserves more than a passing mention'*. So upon his advice I will mention him in more detail.

The Poacher Stories

Kenzie was caught many times in his career and convicted 29 times (charges connected to poaching). He was given considerable fines and had four guns confiscated by local magistrates.

In 1942, Kenzie was declared unfit for military service due to an old wound. That year he had a bumper year for game falling to his gun. The number of game reported is 1,044 head, a mix of partridge, mallard, wigeon, pheasant, geese, shelduck, curlew, hare and even a swan. These were likely to be much appreciated fare at a time of severe rationing.

In fact, such was the demand Kenzie stretched the rules as much as possible and in one outing in the Lincolnshire fens came home with eight swans, taking them home via bicycle.

Kenzie is what I would call a natural poacher - it was an instinctive primal occupation that he could not, even if he had wanted to, resist. He was a survivor and enjoyed the thrill of the hunt, caring little for authority.

Later in life, Kenzie gave up poaching and became a naturalist, goose guide and spare time artist. He lived on a boat made of cedar which was tethered and floated when required. His reputation was widespread after the 1940s and he was in demand to speak about his life as a poacher and as a guide. However, had he been born in the previous century he would surely have been transported to Australia!

Kenzie's Boat

More information about Kenzie can be found in videos made about him at the East Anglian Film Archive and in the renowned book by Colin Willock, *Kenzie The Wild Goose Man* and of course in the aforementioned books by John Humphries and Derek Mills.

Who is the Real Lincolnshire Poacher?

Further stories about specific Lincolnshire poachers, keepers, farmers, landowners and bobbies can be read in Derek Mills' book, '*The Lincolnshire Poachers*'. Whether any of these men know or can be hailed as the True Lincolnshire Poacher is unknown. Maybe, he is a combination of all named and unnamed Lincolnshire Poachers.

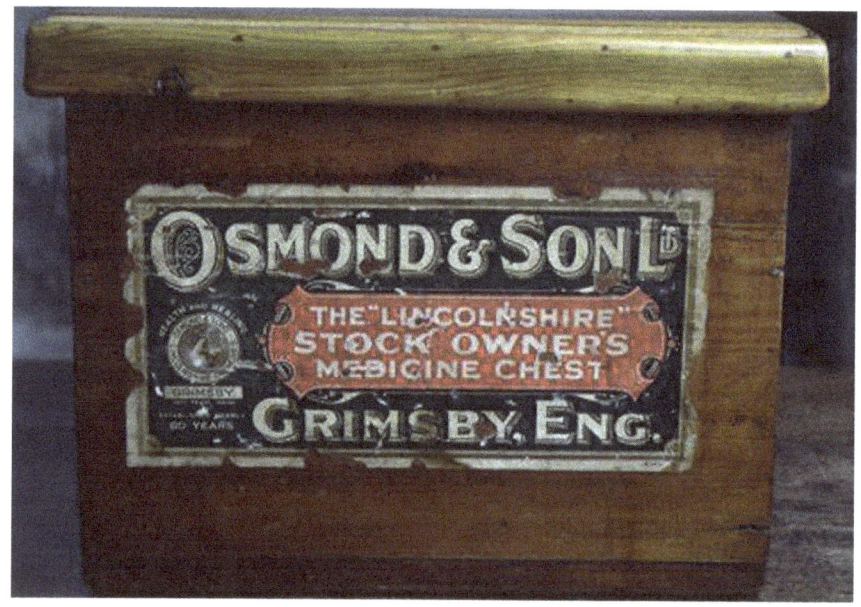

*Osmonds and Sons Medicine Chest
Did cure many an aching or ill.*

8
The Poacher's Parlour

As William Blake stated in his work, Europe: A Prophecy [1], '*Stolen joys are sweet*', and the following dishes will prove thus, reaping the rewards of a poacher's toil.

In the heyday of the poacher, his wife would likely not had scales or a weighing machine and would have produced these recipes from how the ingredients felt and looked at each stage. She may also have substituted different ingredients depending on what was in season or readily available.

Nowadays, we are very fortunate that supermarkets and independent butchers prepare any meat for us. Back in the prime time of the poacher, he and his wife (mainly his wife) would have been highly proficient at preparing any game. This would have involved; plucking feathers or skinning fur, removing entrails and releasing stomach contents, jointing, spatching and trussing followed by cooking and finally the delight of eating.

Poacher's Pie (or Rabbit Pie)

This is a version of a very ancient 'Poachers Pie' which has a topping of bread slices.

1 rabbit, jointed

Seasoned flour (salt and pepper)

1 oz dripping

2 carrots, sliced

1½ pints beef stock

Salt and black pepper

4 oz mushrooms, wiped and thickly sliced

1 large onion, peeled and thickly sliced

3 large slices white bread (crusts on), thickly cut

Chopped fresh parsley to garnish

Set oven to 350°F or Gas Mark 4. Dust the rabbit joints with seasoned flour. Melt the dripping in a large pan and fry the joints all over to brown. Add the onion and carrots, pour over the stock, season to taste and bring to the boil. Transfer the whole to a casserole dish, cover and cook for 1-1½ hours until the rabbit joints are tender. Add the mushrooms. Cut the bread slices in half diagonally and dip one side into the gravy. Place on top of the casserole mixture, gravy side up, and cook in the oven for a further 40 minutes, uncovered, until the bread has become crisp. Serve sprinkled with chopped parsley and accompanied with boiled potatoes. Serves 4.

Poacher's Soup

A lovely, rich country soup which uses the left-overs from any kind of game; pheasant, partridge, rabbit, hare etc.

Carcasses of cooked game
Scraps of cooked game meat
2 medium carrots, roughly chopped
1 tbsp bacon fat or oil
2 large onions, roughly chopped
1 small turnip, roughly chopped
1 stick celery, chopped
1 bay leaf
Sprig of fresh thyme
8 peppercorns
3 pints vegetable stock
1-2 tbsps sherry
2 fl.oz double cream for serving

First heat the fat or oil in a large saucepan. Add the vegetables, cover and cook gently for 5 minutes, taking care not to let them brown. Remove from the heat. Add the broken up carcasses, the herbs and peppercorns and the stock, but reserve a little stock for blending. Bring to the boil, cover and simmer for 2-3 hours until the stock is really well flavoured. Strain and return to the saucepan. In a blender or food processor, purée the scraps of meat with a little of the reserved stock until smooth. Return to the pan with any remaining stock. Season and bring to the boil so that the meat is well heated through. Stir in the sherry (amount according to preference) and serve with a swirl of double cream in each bowl. Serves 6.

Cooking Rabbit

It is advised you should always cook rabbit long enough so you are able to remove the entire skeleton in one piece.

Important Tip: Before cooking rabbit, check the liver. If the liver is spotted it should **not** be eaten. This spotting is an early indication of myxomatosis.

Didn't like rabbit

Some people who visited us said they didn't like rabbit, but that was all we had to give them. We used to tell them it was the dark meat from the chicken or an old cockerel or something like that – they tucked into it and enjoyed it.

Game Pie

Pheasant or partridge with steak and bacon form the basis of this substantial pie.

1 pheasant or a brace partridge, cleaned and jointed
8 oz stewing steak, cut into 1 inch cubes
Seasoned flour (salt and pepper)
2 rashers streaky bacon, cut into strips
1 oz butter
1 onion, peeled and chopped
1 oz button mushrooms, wiped
A bouquet garni
Salt and black pepper
1 pint prepared brown stock
10 oz shortcrust pastry or flaky pastry
1 beaten egg

Set the oven to 300°F or Gas Mark 2. Melt the butter in a pan and fry the onion until just soft; remove and set aside. Dust the steak with seasoned flour, brown lightly in the pan and place in the bottom of a deep pie dish. Repeat with the pheasant or partridge joints, place them on top of the steak, and then scatter over the reserved onion, the bacon strips and mushrooms. Add the herbs and season to taste. Pour on sufficient stock to cover, then cover the dish with kitchen foil and cook for 1½-2 hours. Remove from the oven and allow to cool. Increase heat to 400°F or Gas Mark 6. Remove the herbs and discard, then add sufficient stock to bring the level to ½ an inch from the top of the filling. Roll out the pastry, on a floured surface, cover the pie and trim. Decorate and brush with a beaten egg. Bake for 20 minutes, then reduce oven to 300°F or Gas Mark 2 and bake for a further 15 minutes or until the pie is golden. Serves 4 to 6.

When I make game pie, I may add cranberries for some sweetness. My test to find good butcher is always to try their game pie, it never fails.

Woodpigeon with Mushrooms

Woodpigeons have long been shot by farmers as they are an enduring pest. Although taking some time to cook, their slightly gamey flavour makes a tasty casserole.

4 woodpigeons, prepared

2 oz butter

2 tablespoons oil

2 medium onions, sliced

8 oz mushrooms, halved

1 large cooking apple, peeled, cored and sliced

2 tbsp cranberry jelly

1 bay leaf

¼ pint chicken stock

1 cup cider

1 heaped dessertspoon cornflour

Salt and pepper

Heat the butter and oil in a large, flameproof casserole dish on the hob and brown the birds all over. Remove and set aside. Lower the heat and fry the onions until lightly browned. Remove from the heat and add the mushrooms, apple slices, cranberry jelly and bay leaf and season well. Place the pigeons on the mixture and pour over the stock and cider. Bring to the boil, cover and simmer for 2-2½ hours, stirring occasionally. When the pigeons are tender, remove and set aside. Remove the bay leaf. Drain off the liquid into a pan and stir in the cornflour, already mixed with a little water. Bring to the boil, stirring until the liquid thickens. Return the gravy to the casserole with the pigeons, stir well and finally heat through gently. Serves 4.

Pheasant and Apple Stew

Use Egremont Russet* apples (or similar) to give the stew a spicy apple flavour.

2 lb Egremont Russet apples

1 pheasant, prepared

2 oz butter

1 onion, peeled and chopped

4 juniper berries

Pinch of dried thyme

1 bay leaf

1 glass of apple juice

Salt and pepper

Melt the butter in a large saucepan and sauté the pheasant until brown all over. Meanwhile, peel and core the apples and leave them whole. When the pheasants are browned, add the chopped onion, berries, herbs and seasoning, pour in the apple juice and surround the pheasant with the whole apples. Bring to the boil, cover the pan and simmer until the pheasant is tender. When cooked, remove the pheasant and apples to a serving dish and keep warm. Boil down the pan juices and thicken with a little cornflour blended with a little cold water to make the gravy. Serve with roast potatoes or game chips and a green vegetable. Serves 2.

* It is sometimes said that Egremont Russet apples have the best flavour of all the apple varieties. One pilot study also suggests this old Victorian variety has more phloridzin than newer, shiny-skinned equivalents. Phloridzin is thought to reduce the risk of Type 2 diabetes.

Jugged Hare

The name comes from the lidded stoneware jug in which this dish was originally cooked. A normal casserole dish with a lid will do equally well. Caution: this recipe is very much an acquired taste.

1 hare, prepared and cut into joints
Seasoned flour (salt and pepper)
1 onion, peeled and studded with cloves
1 small orange, wiped and quartered
2½ oz butter
1 carrot, sliced
1 stick of celery, sliced
A bouquet garni
4 peppercorns
1 pint beef stock
2 tablespoons redcurrant jelly
4 fl.oz wine or port
Salt and pepper
Butter and flour for thickening
Pinch of ground mace and nutmeg

Set oven to 350°F or Gas Mark 4. Toss the hare joints in seasoned flour. Melt the ½ oz butter in a large frying pan and brown the joints quickly all over. Remove from the pan and put into a large casserole dish with the onion, carrot, celery, orange, bouquet garni and spices. Pour over the stock, bring to the boil, cover tightly and simmer for about 3 hours. When the meat is tender, transfer to a serving dish and keep hot. To thicken the gravy, melt 2 oz of butter in a pan and stir in 1½ oz of flour. Add the strained liquid from the casserole and bring to the boil, stirring until thickened. Stir in the redcurrant jelly and wine/port and re-heat but do not boil. Pour the thickened gravy over the meat in the dish. Serve with forcemeat balls and croutons together with jacket potatoes and green vegetables. Serves 4 to 6.

Pigeon or Rook Stew

Rooks have a more subtle flavour than pigeons and are more 'gamey'. Most game dealers don't seem to sell them these days but I have seen them available at game fairs. They are impossibly fiddly to pluck. For this reason I suggest you skin them rather than attempt it, then remove the head and backbone as they give a bitter and unpleasant taste.

4 wood pigeons (or rooks) plucked and prepped for the pot

1 sliced onion (or ramsons*) left overnight with a sprinkling of brown sugar

Several large cubes of bacon scraps or salt pork

A large bunch of hedgerow herbs such as chives, chervil, marjoram and sorrel

Salt and pepper

A dash of mushroom ketchup

1 pint of water

1 pint of blackberry or other red wine

Mixture of root vegetables, carrots, parsnips, turnip, all diced

Put all the ingredients into the casserole dish and seal the lid on with a strip of flour and water paste. Bring to a high temperature and then cook in a hay pit or a slow cooker for 4-5 hours. Return to the fire for 20 minutes before serving. Serve with floury boiled potatoes. Alternatively, cook conventionally on the top of the stove and simmer in a sealed pot for 1½-2 hours until tender. Serves 2 to 4.

* Ramsons (allium ursinum) is also known as wild garlic, buckrams, wood garlic, bear leek or bears garlic. Ramsons can be found in plentiful supply in Lincolnshire woodland.

Mustard Rabbit

Rabbit meat and pork casserole with a rich and creamy mustard sauce.

1 young rabbit, cleaned and jointed

Seasoned flour (mustard powder, salt and pepper)

A little cooking oil

½ lb belly pork, skinned, boned and cubed

2 carrots, sliced

1 large onion, chopped

1 tbsp chopped fresh parsley

2 tsp chopped fresh thyme

1 bay leaf

Salt and black pepper

½ pint dry cider

Chicken stock

3 egg yolks

¼ pint double cream

1 level tbsp dry Colman's® Mustard Powder

Chopped fresh parsley for garnish

Set oven to 350° F or Gas Mark 4. Coat the rabbit pieces with seasoned flour. Heat the oil in a large pan and lightly fry the rabbit joints. Place half the pork and half the vegetables in a casserole dish and lay the rabbit joints on top. Add the herbs and seasoning and top with remaining pork and vegetables. Pour the cider into the pan and bring to the boil. Pour into the casserole dish with sufficient hot stock just to cover. Cover the dish with a lid and cook for 1½-2 hours until tender. Remove the meat and vegetables to a warm serving dish and keep hot. Strain the liquid into a pan and boil hard to reduce. Beat together the egg yolks, cream and mustard powder, add 3-4 tbsp of the reduced liquid and whisk. Pour into the remainder of the liquid and heat through thoroughly. Take care not to let it boil or the sauce will curdle.

Adjust the seasoning, adding more mustard if necessary, then spoon over the rabbit. Garnish with parsley and serve with creamed potatoes and green vegetables. Serves 4 to 6.

I would always use Colman's® Mustard Powder as Reckitt and Colman once grew some of their mustard in Lincolnshire soil.

Rabbit and Apple Stew

A simple way to convert rabbit joints into a tasty meal.

1 6 joints of rabbit
Seasoned flour (salt and pepper)
2 oz butter
2 medium onions, chopped
2 medium carrots, sliced
2 medium apples, peeled, cored and thickly sliced
8 oz mushrooms sliced
8 oz streaky bacon, cut into 1 inch pieces
½ pint vegetable stock
2 tsp tomato purée
Sprig of fresh thyme or 1 tsp dried thyme
Salt and pepper

Heat half the butter in a large saucepan and cook the onions, carrots, and apples for 5 minutes, stirring well. Remove from the pan and set aside. Toss the rabbit joints in the seasoned flour. Heat the remaining butter in the pan and brown the rabbit joints on both sides. Lower the heat, add the mushrooms and bacon pieces and continue cooking for 5 minutes. Add the stock slowly and then add the reserved apple/vegetable mixture, the tomato purée and thyme, stirring all the time and season. Bring to the boil, cover, lower the heat and simmer for 1 hour or until the rabbit is tender. Stir occasionally and add more stock or boiling water if required. Serves 4 to 6.

Game Stew

Use any variety and mixture of game meat to make this flavoursome stew.

1 lb mixed game meat: grouse, venison, hare etc.
2 oz ham, diced
Seasoned flour (salt and pepper)
2 oz butter
1 small onion, peeled and chopped
1 carrot, chopped
2 sticks celery, chopped
¾ pint game or beef stock
3 fl.oz red wine
Salt and pepper

Cut the game meat into cubes and toss in the seasoned flour. Dice the ham. Melt the butter in a heavy bottom casserole dish. Fry the vegetables until soft, then add the game meat and ham, continue frying until browned. Add the stock and red wine. Bring to the boil, cover with a lid and simmer gently for 1-1½ hours, skimming occasionally. Season and serve with mashed potato and redcurrant or rowan jelly. Serves 4.

Savoury Leek Pudding

This was a real hard times pudding, but one that we enjoyed nonetheless.

8 oz self-raising flour
3 oz suet
Water
3 or 4 leeks, washed, trimmed and sliced
A handful of pignuts* or parsnips, diced and chopped
Ends of left-over cheese, chopped
1 or 2 rashers of bacon, finely chopped
A handful of filberts, if available
Mixed dried or fresh herbs

Make up the suet pastry by mixing the flour and suet to a thick paste with a little cold water. Roll out into a circle on a floured board and cut out a quarter segment. Use the main part to line a greased 2 pint pudding basin. Press the edges together and then fill with all the other ingredients. Wet the top edges of the pastry and then fit the lid using the remaining pastry, sealing in all the ingredients. Cover the whole pudding with greaseproof paper, being sure to fold the paper into a pleat in the middle to allow for expansion. Cover with a pudding cloth and tie the paper and the cloth round the basin tightly with string to prevent any water getting into the pudding (or seal with kitchen foil). Steam for 2-3 hours in a saucepan, topping up the water as necessary, serve with a parsley sauce. Serves 4.

* Pignuts are a woodland plant with a small edible root. They are common but hard to find due to their size. They take a long time to grow and produce a tuber so should only be picked if found in profusion. Also known as arnuts, earth chestnuts, ground nuts or kipper nuts.

Sorrel Sauce

The sharp, lemony tang of sorrel makes a perfect sauce for pork and duck, or any rich, fat meat. It is made in a matter of minutes, without any of the problems associated with sauce making. Makes about ½ pint of sauce.

2 lb of sorrel leaves
Butter
Freshly milled black pepper

Wash the sorrel leaves and put them damp in a saucepan. Cook for 5 minutes, drain and return to the pan with the butter and pepper. Beat to a purée with a wooden spoon and serve hot.

Sorrel-stuffed Fish.

A friend of mine, Jenny, made us a fish pie once. Steve, another pal, caught this really big pike and he didn't really want to kill it, he wanted to put it back but it died on him. So he took it to Jenny and Jenny sorted it all out! It was the best tasting pie I'd ever had, but the problem with pike is it has tiny bones. It takes ages to take them out.

However, I have been told the French have a recipe that may solve this issue. If you have a bony fish to cook, stuff it with sorrel leaves and wrap it in foil. The acid in the sorrel will melt the bones of the fish. so you are able to eat without the fear of choking on a bone.

Taste of Sorrel

When we were younger, if we came across a clump of sorrel, we would pick a few leaves to chew for its lemony taste. Our Uncle George said the reason it tasted so good was a dog had come across the clump and cocked his leg to wee on it.

Lincolnshire Poacher Cheese

A world-renowned, award-winning cheese that seems as though it has been around for centuries yet has only been in production since 1992. It was first created by Simon Jones at his family farm, Ulceby Grange, near Alford on the very cusp of the Lincolnshire Wolds.

Simon, upon returning from agricultural college, looked into cheese making on a small scale and with the help of Welsh cheese maker, Dougal Campbell, he made his first batch of cheese on February 17th, 1992. Initially, the cheese lacked a name but Richard Jones, Simon's father came up with the name, using inspiration from the unofficial anthem of Lincolnshire. He felt it would resonate well with local people.

The cheese is made using traditional methods with the unpasteurised milk from the farm's 230 Holstein Fresian Cows. The recipe is said to be a cross between a traditional West Country cheddar and a continental alpine cheese, with small technical variances to provide a unique texture and flavour.

If you would like to know more about Lincolnshire Poacher Cheese please visit https://lincolnshirepoachercheese.com.

Lincolnshire Stuffed Chine®

Lincolnshire Stuffed Chine is a cured cut of pork, slashed and stuffed with parsley. In the past, it would have been stuffed with whatever leaves were in season such as sharp stinging nettles. Originally, the Lincolnshire Curly Coat pig would have been killed and prepared. Chine is an acquired taste with its detractors referring to it as 'Ham and Hedge-cuttings'. Lincolnshire Stuffed Chine was reserved for celebrations such as May Hiring Fairs and christenings.

The Kitchen Range

In Victorian times, a 'Kitchen Range' was at the centre of family life, providing cooking facilities, hot water and heating. If the poacher was lucky his house would have a range, else he and his wife would have to make do with cooking over an open fire.

A kitchen range would usually be made from cast iron and came in many shapes and sizes. Whatever the size, a range consisted of the same essential parts: a flue (with dampers), hinged door coal compartment, a sliding grate (to remove the ashes), top plate and closed oven compartments which had varied temperatures.

The fire which heated the range ran on coal and was kept on all the time. Whenever the range was needed for cooking or baking, not just heating, its fire needed to be stoked up well in advance. Recognising a *'suitable'* temperature required great skill and experience as there were no oven thermostats. Kept near the oven would be bellows and a poker for easy accessibility to stoke the oven. Working near a kitchen range could be hot, sweaty and very uncomfortable.

The range would have to be regularly emptied of ash, coal loaded and the surfaces kept clean. This job regularly fell to young children. Cleaning the exposed surfaces was done using a polish known as *'black lead'* and wire wool.

A range is still popular today though it now has all the *'mod-cons'* including thermostats and some even operate using electricity.

Upon the kitchen range there hung,
A kettle with a rabbit hid under the lid.

9
The Poacher's Property

A fine testament to the Lincolnshire Poacher is the number of buildings, locations and property, such public houses and inns, which proudly bear his name. He has even inspired a section of railway which is now dedicated to him.

I have attempted to compile a list of these as a way to further honour him. I am sure there are many I have missed despite fervent searches and requests for information. I would like to add more to this chapter, so if you know of other real estate or properties named after the Lincolnshire Poacher then please get it touch so it may be included in future editions.

The Lincolnshire Poacher, Bunkers Hill

An old traditional pub that welcomes everyone: families, couples and beer-lovers. Offers a selection of real ales and serves a wide variety of food, including pub classics such as fish and chips, burger, curries, steak and Hunter's chicken. On Sundays, they offer a generous carvery.

One of those warm, friendly village pubs which make you smile the minute you walk in. Outside boasts a patio with log burner and children's play area.

The Lincolnshire Poacher
Bunkers Hill
Lincoln
LN2 4QT

The Lincolnshire Poacher, Spalding

After a long walk in the surrounding countryside, this Lincolnshire Poacher is a great pub to visit. The intimate atmosphere of this venue allows guests to relax after a hard working day. Here they offer traditional British cuisine in a relaxed setting.

The Lincolnshire Poacher
11 Double Street
Spalding
PE11 2AA

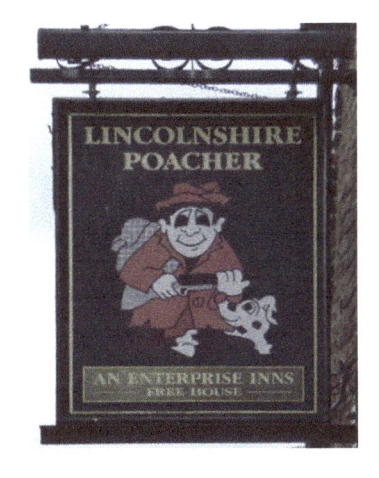

The Lincolnshire Poacher, Metheringham

This charming B&B is set in the quaint village of Metheringham, 15 minutes' drive from the centre of Lincoln. It offers cosy accommodation with free Wi-Fi, full English breakfasts and a traditional pub serving homemade meals, specialising in steaks and traditional British cuisine made with local produce.

The Lincolnshire Poacher
53 High Street
Metheringham
Lincoln
LN4 3DS

The Lincolnshire Poacher, Nottingham

A vital part of Nottingham's real ale scene which offers a variety of high quality real ale. This Poacher also cooks up delicious fresh food everyday. It has a large bar and a function room, which can seat up to 40 guests.

Lincolnshire Poacher
161-163 Mansfield Road
Nottingham
NG1 3FR

Other Poacher Signs

Here are photos of other Lincolnshire Poacher pub signs from Stamford, Lincolnshire, taken between 1970 and 1980. These pubs have now been renamed.

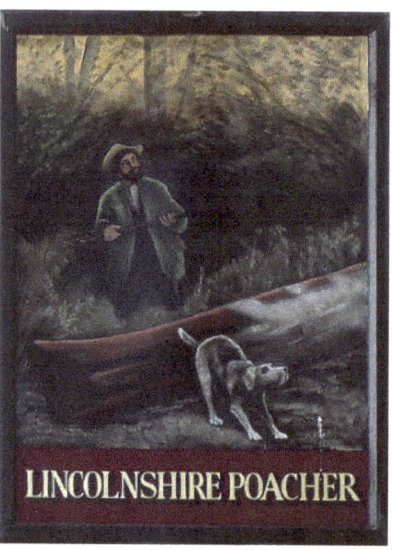

There once was a pub called the Lincolnshire Poacher in Louth, situated on Eastgate. It was a traditional style inn with a bar restaurant and had a guest house.

This beautifully painted sign was the Louth pub sign. It is now displayed in an antiques store in Louth. The proprietor will not part with it, much to my disappointment! The original pub building is now a residential property.

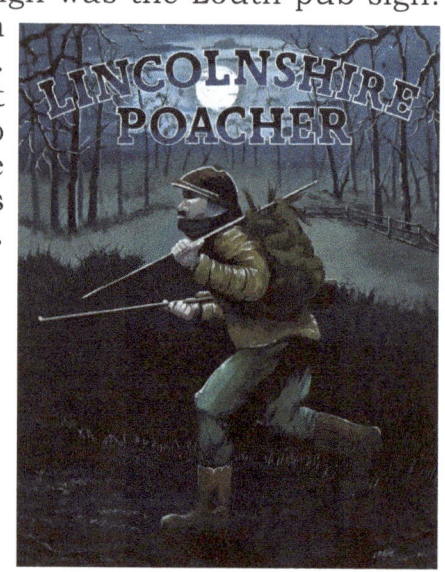

The Poacher Line

The Grantham-Skegness train line, originally promoted as *'The Poacher Line'*, runs for 55 miles (89km). Trains on this route originate from Nottingham via the Nottingham to Grantham Line as an hourly through service from Nottingham to Skegness, with slower stopping services at peak times. The line is operated by East Midlands Railway, and the British Rail Class 153, 156 'Super-Sprinter' and British Rail Class 158 'Sprinter Express', all diesel multiple units run on it. On a rare occasion (Summer Saturdays only) a British Rail Class 43 (HST) will also run on the line.

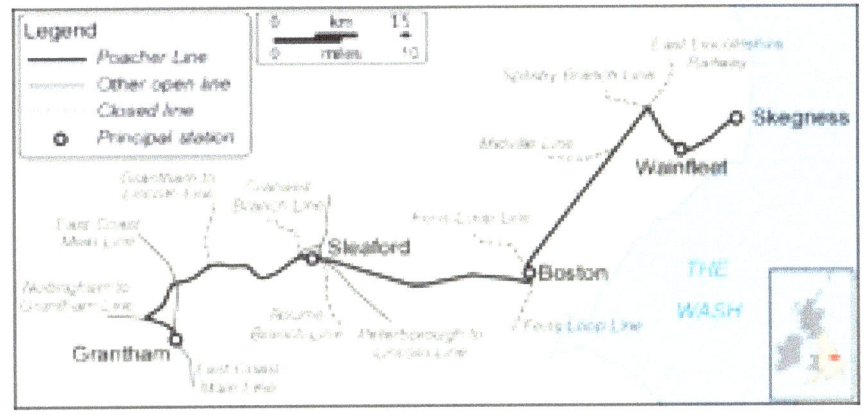

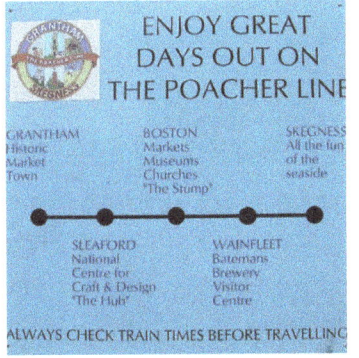

Along the route you will find quaint market towns including; Grantham, Sleaford and Boston. The journey ends at the seaside town of Skegness, which boasts long sandy beaches and traditional seaside attractions.

The logo of *The Poacher Line* is a pheasant's silhouette.

Lincolnshire Poacher 80080 Train

On 3rd June 1989, an 80080 train named *'The Lincolnshire Poacher'* toured from St Pancras to Lincoln Central.

This image was taken at Nottingham while the train was taking on water. Other Lincolnshire Poacher trains include an Immingham to Southampton train in 1961 and Immingham to London in 2003.

Commemorative Benches

Around the county there are numerous benches dedicated to soldiers lost in the Great Wars. The 2nd Battalion The Royal Anglian Regiment, known as *'The Poachers'* have one such bench in Clecthorpes, Lincolnshire.

As they lay and now rest,
Sit ye here and remember them.

10
The Lincolnshire Poacher Song

The Lincolnshire Poacher is possibly most well known in the form of a song or poem. It is considered to be the unofficial county anthem of Lincolnshire. It is catalogued in the Roud Folk Song Index as No. 299. This index is a database of around 250,00 songs collected from oral tradition in the English language.

The song was the Regimental Quick March of the 10th Regiment of Foot and consequently its successors, the Royal Lincolnshire Regiment and the 2nd Battalion Royal Anglian Regiment who are known as *'The Poachers'*. The Regimental Band and Corps of Drums have recorded the song on their album *'Oh, It's My Delight'*.

Today, the 2nd Battalion Royal Anglian Regiment are a Light Mechanised Infantry Battalion, part of 7th Infantry Brigade and 1st (UK) Division. They recruit from across the East of England (including Lincolnshire) and are based right in the heartland of their recruiting area, Kendrew Barracks, Rutland.

The Lincolnshire Poacher

When I was bound apprentice, in famous Lincolnshire
Full well I served my master for more than seven year
Till I took up to poaching as you shall quickly hear;
Oh! 'tis my delight on a shining night
in the season of the year.
Oh! 'tis my delight on a shining night
in the season of the year.

As me and my companions were setting of a snare,
'Twas when we spied the gamekeeper, for him we did not care,
For we can wrestle & fight, my boys, & jump o'er anywhere;
Oh! 'tis my delight etc..

As me and my companions were setting four or five,
And taking on 'em up again, we caught a hare alive;
We took the hare alive, my boys, & through the woods did steer;
Oh! 'tis my delight etc..

I took him on my shoulder, & then we trudged home,
We took him to a neighbour's house & sold him for a crown,
We sold him for a crown, my boys, I did not tell you where;
Oh! 'tis my delight etc..

Success to every gentleman who lives in Lincolnshire,
Success to every poacher who wants to sell a hare,
Bad luck to every gamekeeper who will not sell his deer;
Oh! 'tis my delight etc..

In addition to this, the song is the principal musical theme of the quick march of the Intelligence Corps. Prior to 1881, they were known as the 81st Regiment of Foot (Loyal Lincoln Volunteers).

When the Royal Air Force College Cranwell, the Officer Training Academy of the Royal Air Force, was formed in Lincolnshire in 1919, its first Commandant, Air Commodore C.A.H. Longcroft, sought permission from the then Regimental Colonel of the Royal Lincolnshire Regiment to adopt the march as the quick march of the College.

Overseas Battalions

During the American Civil War, many New York Regiments used the tune, renaming it as The New York Volunteer.

During the First World War, the 20th Battalion, Australian Imperial Force used The Lincolnshire Poacher as their marching song.

The Lincoln and Welland Regiment of Canadian Forces use the song as their authorised march.

Number Stations

The Lincolnshire Poacher song was transmitted from the shortwave radio number station E03. It was used as the opening interval and made to sound like a calliope machine (a musical instrument that produces sound by sending compressed air through large whistles - made popular in traditional circus carousels). After the song, a machine-made female voice would read a 5 digit call up. Station E03 is widely believed to have been run by the British Secret Intelligence Service. It was first broadcast from Bletchley Park in the mid-1970s but later broadcasted from RAF Akrotiri in Cyprus.

King George IV

The earliest printed version of the song appeared in York about 1776, and the song is thought to have been a favourite of King George IV. Many other counties have transformed it into their dialects, such as Somerset, Northumberland and Leicestershire but it properly belongs to Lincolnshire.

Popular Music

The popularity of the tune has continued in various guises. In 1950, a novelty song called *'The Thing'* by Phil Harris used the melody and reached number one in the US charts. In 1961, Benjamin Britten arranged the song as No.3 in Volume 5 of British Folk Songs.

The Brighouse and Rastrick Brass Band used The Lincolnshire Poacher as their follow up single to *'The Floral Dance'* and it is included on their 1978 album.

American metal-core band Norma Jean released an album in 2016 called *Polar Similar*. One of the tracks samples a parody of the Lincolnshire Poacher number station signal.

Radio Lincolnshire

Radio Lincolnshire used the melody from the chorus as the news jingle from 1980-1988. The station continues to use a version with a less pronounced melody today.

On the Screen

In the 1940 film, *Tom Brown's School Days*, the Rugby School students sang the melody of the song. It is also the theme song of the movie.

In October 2020, an Amazon Original Series called *Truth Seekers* created a mysterious supernatural event based on the number station broadcast of the Lincolnshire Poacher. In episode seven, 'The Hinckley Boy', the spirit in the machine is a soldier who felt he had failed his country and the central characters help to release him. However, the Lincolnshire Poacher broadcast is a feature that stretches out throughout the series. The series stars Nick Frost, Simon Pegg and Nat Saunders.

Podcast

The Lincolnshire Poacher numbers station features prominently in the second series of the BBC's Lovecraft Investigations podcast '*The Whisperer in Darkness*' starring Jana Carpenter and Barnaby Kay. The are 9 episodes to this chapter of the podcast which can be found on the BBC Radio 4 webpage.

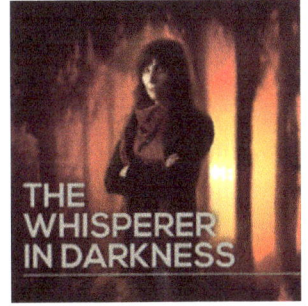

Local Artists

Many local folk singers will choose to sing *'The Lincolnshire Poacher'* when performing a set in a local Lincolnshire village pub as it is sure to be a firm favourite with the punters, and bound to have them joining in.

One enterprising group of Lincolnshire lads have produced an album which hits the very core of Lincolnshire Life. The Ruffs, made up of Glynn, Mick and Trevor, state *"The songs we write are about where we live and things that happen around us."* Some of the tracks on their *'Best Of The Ruffs'* album are: *Rabbit Pie, Inbred and Proud, The Billinghay Ruff* and *Lincoln's Pride*. I have no doubt that when performing they can easily be convinced to sing a round of *The Lincolnshire Poacher*!

Oh! 'tis my delight on a shining night
In the season of the year.

11
The Popular Poacher

The Lincolnshire Poacher has inspired many people from many avenues, some in a conventional manner and others in less usual, unexpected ways.

Lincolnshire Poacher County Magazine

In 1900, the name of the Poacher was used as the title of the county's newly launched magazine. The more modern version of the Lincolnshire Poacher Magazine reappeared in the 1950s and was re-launched in 1996 as an annual publication. Its popularity meant it soon became a quarterly magazine packed with article, stories and poems about life in Lincolnshire.

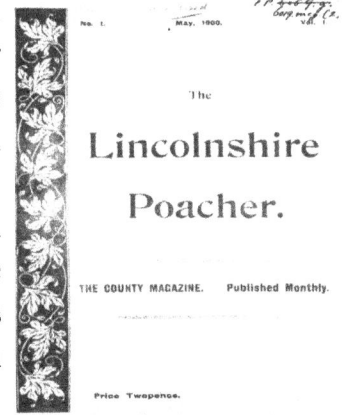

North Kesteven Coat of Arms

The arms were officially granted in 1950. A green shield bears a pale ermine stripe with a pattern of black shapes (representing the winter coat of a stoat), this has added significance as the Roman Road, Ermine Street, runs the length of Kesteven. Placed on top of the ermine is an oak tree for the ancient forests of the County.

Standing on the crest is a Heron with a pike in its beak, for the area's varied wildlife.

The dexter (right-hand side) supporter is a Roman soldier, a reminder of the many Roman antiquities of the County. The sinister (left-hand side) supporter is a poacher. He represents the famous song 'The Lincolnshire Poacher', the unofficial anthem of the County.

The poacher looks to be carrying a sling or a net in his left hand and has a rabbit attached to his belt. In my opinion he looks far too well dressed to be a poacher!

RNLI Lifeboat

In March 1989 a huge fundraising campaign was launched to raise £600,000 required for a new lifeboat and boathouse for Skegness. As the people and businesses of Lincolnshire raised the funds, it seemed appropriate to name the new Lifeboat 'Lincolnshire Poacher'.

The Lincolnshire all-weather lifeboat is a Mersey class lifeboat and arrived in Skegness on 31st July 1990. A naming ceremony and service of dedication for the lifeboat took place on Sunday 30th September 1990. The new boathouse was also formally opened by Mr Michael Vernon, Chairman of the RNLI and Mrs Lucille Van Geest officially handed over Lincolnshire Poacher into the care of Skegness lifeboat station. After the ceremony, a brief demonstration of the new boat's capabilities took place.

A Rose by Any Other Name

A yellow blend hybrid tea rose was bred in the UK by George W.T. Langdale in 1992. For the exhibition he named it *'Lincolnshire Poacher'*. It blooms in flushes throughout the rose flowering season and reaches the height of 32-39 inches.

A Day at the Races

Once a year, *'The International Lincolnshire Poacher'*, a motorcycle meet, is run by the Wainfleet Club at Thorpe St. Peter, near Skegness. It is considered the country's premier grasstrack event and is run over a 1000 metre longtrack. This high-adrenalin spectacle has taken place since 1992 and it attracts international riders from all over the world. The thrilling races include: 1000cc sidecar, 500cc solos and 500cc sidecar events. It is an action packed day out, suitable for the whole family to attend.

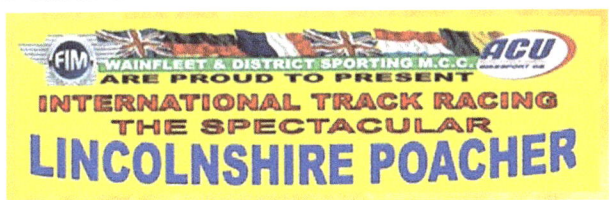

Gravestones

Families sometimes request *'The Lincolnshire Poacher'* to be engraved upon headstones of deceased family members. Whether this is as a nod to the family member being inclined to poach or to acknowledge military service is known only to those who remember the family member. This headstone can be found at the church in the village of Mareham-le-Fen.

*Upon the table lay dead and caught
A welcome sight for supper.*

12
The Poacher's Glossary

Many of the terms or words used by the Lincolnshire Poacher are from another time, long, long ago, and have fallen out of general usage. Other words are taken from the local slang or dialect and have evolved as language does, either due to laziness or an active decision by the poacher to confuse or distract those who may be listening in, trying to catch him.

Word	Meaning
Bagging	Loose netting.
Bassin	A brown, waterproof material similar to moleskin, which blended in well with the environment.
Beaters	People who drive game for open shooting or coursing.
Brace	A pair of something, such as birds or small mammals in hunting.
Charley	An old colloquial term for a fox, used in Lincolnshire and other counties.

Word	Meaning
Chine	An old English word for backbone, derived from Norman French.
Clap net	A spring loaded net.
Coney/Conie	Old terminology for a rabbit. The term has been used in the bible and other old texts.
Covert	Pronounced 'cover', a place of safety or refuge for game.
Covey	A small flock.
Drag Net	A net about 25 yards wide and 4 yards deep, which is dragged over stubble and grass to trap game.
Fenn Trap	A spring loaded, mechanical trap. A modern version of a gin trap (now banned).
Filbert	Another name for hazelnut.
Forcemeat	A highly seasoned mixture containing chopped meat, used as stuffing.
Funnel Net	A net shaped like a funnel, wider at one end and tapering off. Used to trap fish.
Gamechips	They are thin slices of potato or other root vegetables (sometimes dusted with flour; often crinkle-cut), deep-fried, and may be served hot or cold.
Ganzie	A distinctive woollen sweater, originally designed to provide protection for fishermen from wind and water.
Gin trap	A mechanical trap with jaws and teeth to trap a variety of animals.
Hind	A female deer.
Hingle	A snare made of wire and attached to a stake in the ground.
Hob	A male ferret.

Word	Meaning
Huvver	A small strip of land, approximately 1-2 feet wide, between a ploughed furrow and the dyke which stands proud of the soil.
Jill	A female ferret.
Jug or Jugging	Roost or roosting, usually in reference to partridge or pheasant.
Lazey Men	Poachers.
Long Nets	Adjustable nets up to 4-5 feet high and up to 150 yards long, usually used for netting rabbit and hare.
Lure	A man-made imitation of game, covered with feathers or fur, often with a squeaking device inside.
Magnofogler	An old Lincolnshire word for a person who invents or innovates.
Man-trap	A trap used as a deterrent for poachers.
Myxomatosis	An infectious viral disease affecting rabbits.
Nut Stick	A straight stick from a Hazel tree.
Pot-hunter	Poacher.
Pricker Stick	A stick used as a stake for a snare or hingle to hold it off the ground.
Privy	A term for a toilet.
Purse Net	A net with a draw-string, used when ferreting for rabbits.
Roost	Birds settling down for the night/a place where they settle.
Slip Snare	Similar to a hingle.
Spring Gun	Another term for a man-trap.
Yellowbellies	People born and bred in Lincolnshire.

*By the huvver, they feed unaware
As the drag net silently creeps over the stubble.*

List of Organisations

A considerable proportion of this book would not be possible without referring to a large number of organisations or groups. Here I provide a list of the organisations named in the text and their addresses or websites, where available.

Organisation	Address
2nd Battalion The Royal Anglian Regiment 'The Poachers'	Kendrew Barracks, Cottesmore Road, Cottesmore, Oakham, Rutland LE15 7BQ https://www.army.mod.uk/who-we-are/corps-regiments-and-units/infantry/royal-anglian-regiment/2nd-battalion-the-royal-anglian-regiment/
BBC Radio Lincolnshire	Newport, Lincoln, Lincolnshire LN1 3XY https://www.bbc.co.uk/programmes/articles/3LnDw5tWL6MnWR7x47JhC0/about-radio-lincolnshire
Bletchley Park	The Mansion, Bletchley Park, Sherwood Drive, Bletchley, Milton Keynes, Buckinghamshire MK3 6EB https://bletchleypark.org.uk/

Organisation	Address
Boss & Co	110 Kew Green, Richmond, London TW9 3AP https://bossguns.com
Brighouse & Rastrick Brass Band (The)	73 Finkil Street Brighouse, West Yorkshire HD6 2NY https://brighouseandrastrick.com/
Churchill Guns	Park Lane, Lane End, High Wycombe, Buckinghamshire HP14 3NS https://www.ejchurchill.com/gun-room/e-j-churchill-guns/
Colman's®	Avian Way, Norwich, Norfolk NR7 9AJ https://www.colmans.co.uk/
Countryside Alliance	51 Grosvenor Gardens, Belgravia, London SW1W 0AU https://www.countryside-alliance.org/
East Anglian Film Archive	The Archive Centre, County Hall, Martineau Lane, Norwich, Norfolk NR1 2DQ http://www.eafa.org.uk/
East Midlands Railway	https://www.eastmidlandsrailway.co.uk/
Elderkins Gunmakers	Broad Street, Spalding, Lincolnshire PE11 1TG http://www.elderkinguns.co.uk/
GCHQ	Hubble Road, Cheltenham, Gloucestershire GL51 0EX https://www.gchq.gov.uk/
Groundswell – Agriculture	Darnalls Hall Farm, Weston, Hitchin, Hertfordshire SG4 7AL https://groundswellag.com/
Holland & Holland	33 Bruton Street, Mayfair, London W1J 6HH https://www.hollandandholland.com/

List of Organisations

Organisation	Address
Imperial War Museum (IWM)	Lambeth Road, London SE1 6HZ https://www.iwm.org.uk/
IXL (George Wosenholm) Knives	Egginton Bros Ltd, 25-31 Allen Street, Sheffield, South Yorkshire S3 7AW https://www.sheffieldcollectableknives.com/
Lincoln Castle	Castle Square, Lincoln, Lincolnshire LN1 3AA https://www.lincolncastle.com/
Lincolnshire Poacher Cheese Company	F W Read & Sons Ltd, Ulceby Grange, Alford, Lincolnshire LN13 0HE https://lincolnshirepoachercheese.com/
Lincolnshire Today Magazine	Armstrong House, Armstrong Street, Grimsby, North East Lincolnshire DN31 2QE https://lincolnshiretoday.net/mag/
MGR Guns	1 Witham Road, Woodhall Spa, Lincolnshire LN10 6RW http://www.mgrguns.co.uk/
Museum of Methodism & John Wesley's House	Wesley's Chapel and Leysian Mission, 49 City Road, London EC1Y 1AU https://www.wesleysheritage.org.uk/
National Gamekeeper's Organisation (The)	PO Box 246, Darlington, County Durham DL1 9FZ https://www.nationalgamekeepers.org.uk/
National Farming Union	Agriculture House, Stoneleigh Park, Stoneleigh, Warwickshire CV8 2TZ https://www.nfuonline.com/
National Union of Agricultural and Allied Workers (NUAW) 1906-1982 now Unite - The Union Rural and Agricultural Sector	Unite House, 128 Theobalds Road, Holborn, London WC1X 8TN https://unitetheunion.org/what-we-do/unite-in-your-sector/rural-and-agricultural/#

Organisation	Address
North Kesteven District Council	District Council Offices, Kesteven Street, Sleaford, Lincolnshire NG34 7EF https://www.n-kesteven.gov.uk/
Osmond's (formerly based in Grimsby)	Bradeley Green, Tarporley Road, Whitchurch, Shropshire SY13 4HD https://www.osmonds.co.uk/
Police and Crime Commissioner	Lincolnshire Police Headquarters, Deepdale Lane, Nettleham, Lincolnshire LN2 2LT https://www.lincs.police.uk/about-us/police-and-crime-commissioner/
Purdey Guns and Rifles	57-58 South Audley Street, London W1K 2ED https://www.purdey.com/
RAF Cranwell	RAF College Cranwell, Sleaford, Lincolnshire NG34 8HB https://www.raf.mod.uk/our-organisation/stations/raf-college-cranwell/
Reckitt (now Reckitt Benckiser)	103-105 Bath Road, Slough, Berkshire SL1 3UH https://www.rb.com/
Royal National Lifeboat Institution (RNLI)	West Quay Road, Poole, Dorset BH15 1HZ https://rnli.org/
Taylor's Eye Witness (Knives)	5 Parkway Close, Sheffield, South Yorkshire S9 4WJ https://taylors-eye-witness.co.uk/
Vaughan Williams Memorial Library (The) The Essential Folk Resource	English Folk Dance and Song Society, Cecil Sharp House, 2 Regent's Park Road, London NW1 7AY https://www.vwml.org/

List of Organisations

Organisation	Address
Vintage Gun Journal (The)	Vintage Guns Ltd, Caynham Court, Caynham, Ludlow, Shropshire, SY8 3BJ https://www.vintageguns.co.uk/magazine
Wainfleet Club	New Farm, Wainfleet Bank, Wainfleet, Skegness, Lincolnshire PE24 4JP http://www.superspeedtrack.com/
Wall Street Journal	1211 Avenue of the Americas, New York 10036 USA https://www.wsj.com/news/magazine
Webley & Scott Gunmakers	Frankly Industrial Park, Tay Road, Rednal, Birmingham B45 0P https://www.webleyandscott.com/
Woodhall Spa 1940's Festival	https://www.facebook.com/WoodhallSpa40sFestival/

*On alert, perhaps he heard a snap
Whilst his harem feast on seeds spread o'er the ground.*

About the Author

David was born in Lincolnshire, within 2 miles of Kirkstead Abbey (as the crow flies). The Tonge family has been farming in the Fens since 1840.

David's Great-Grandfather and Great-Uncle, along with other local farmers, were instrumental in pioneering the drainage of the area. They put a drainage channel through the area which is now the main road of Woodhall Spa.

David believes if he had been born over a hundred years ago he would been known as the local magnafogler, an old Lincolnshire term for someone who invents or innovates. He is keen on developing and investigating new innovations within farming, such as new techniques especially those related to regenerative farming.

He is a proud member of Groundswell, an organisation which provides a forum for farmers interested in food production or the environment to learn about the theory and practical applications of Conservation Agriculture and Regenerative Systems.

David has three children and an Irish Red Setter called Dixie. He is essentially self sufficient on his farm and has chickens, guinea-fowl, pigs and a large vegetable garden, large enough to plough with a Ferguson 135 tractor, so he doesn't have to dig!

When not giving talks on *The Poacher*, David can be found reading in his library, out metal detecting or reclaiming materials from old buildings.

David enjoys this quote by Rick Butts, author and speaker, *'For a person who has never led an army into battle, been elected to higher office, acted in movies or committed a heinous crime, a good book is the way to bridge the credibility gap.'*

David would humbly suggest this quote could be applied to him as author of this book, *'The Lincolnshire Poacher'*.

Acknowledgements

My special thanks to the following who sent me their fascinating reminiscences.

Charles Peace - for his remarkable stories, including the stories from the Wall Street Journal. It is possible to purchase the full article through the Wall Street Journal's website.

John Larder - for granting me permission to use his images of paintings by A.V. Spall.

Richard Wilson of MGR Gun Room of Woodhall Spa for the provision of old shotgun adverts.

Members of the audiences at my talks - you never fail to provide me with new anecdotes.

The knowledgeable gentleman who sells second hand books at Melton Mowbray Market.

All the retired police officers who had run-ins with local poachers and shared these tidbits of information.

An extra special thanks to:

Chris and Sheila Collins of Cherry Willingham, who responded to my request on Radio Lincolnshire for more information on the Poacher. Chris had his own personal database compiled as a labour of love over 12 years. It holds 14,000 names spaced over 700 years. He painstakingly retrieved the names of all the poachers on one of the first computers made in his upstairs room.

To show me how the database worked he put in the surname 'TONGE' - 3 names came up! Swiftly moving on...

After several days he completed the task - the complete list of 'caught poachers' is in the book - and I believe it is the first time it has been presented in a book. I wondered about publishing the tables in case people complained about it besmirching their family's good name. I then thought the opposite might be true, and families would want to know why their relatives are not mentioned!

To the first group, I'd say it is a matter of public record if people care to find out. To the second - your relatives were smart and cunning enough not to get caught! The A team as mentioned in Chapter 6 - The Poacher's Remorse.

Future Editions

This book is by no means all there is to say about the Lincolnshire Poacher, I have tried to include stories and anecdotes not previously written. I know there is much, much more out there, particularly from the poachers and the families of those poachers caught and transported to Virginia, USA, Australia and Gibraltar. Due to a number of reasons people do not talk about these stories, we need to remove the stigma of the topic by talking about them. Their stories deserve to be heard.

The Chinese have a saying, 'Every time a person dies; a public library closes.' If you want to share your reminiscences of the Lincolnshire Poacher, please get in touch, I would very much love to hear them - they could even be included in the next edition of this book to make it even better and brighter.

If you enjoyed this book, please add a review on Amazon for me.

References

Books

Archer, Fred, *Poacher's Pie*, (Hodder and Stoughton Paperbacks), 1976

Blake, William, *Europe: A Prophecy [1]*, (CreateSpace Independent Publishing Platform), 2015

Cobbett, William, *Rural Rides*, (Penguin Classics), 2001

Cuthbert, Robert, Eastham, Jake and Parle, Andy, *A Hunter's Step-by-Step Guide to Cooking Game,* (Hermes House, Anness Publishing Ltd), 2010

Editors of Grit Magazine, *Lard: The Lost Art of Cooking with your Grandma's Secret Ingredient*, (Andrew McMeel Publishing), 2012

Horwitz, Tony, *Very Dark Plots Are Afoot in England, As Grouse Grow Fat - It's Gamekeeper vs. Poacher In An Old Feudal Rite*, (Wall Street Journal), 1991

Humphries, John, *Poacher Tales*, (David & Charles plc), 1993

Kirkman, F.B. and Jourdain, F.C.R., *British Birds*, (Thomas Nelson and Sons Ltd), 1950

Lawrence, D.H., *Lady Chatterley's Lover*, (Harper Collins), 2013

Mcneaney, Sean, *Murdered by Poachers*, (The Lincolnshire Poacher), 2014

Mills, Derek, *The Lincolnshire Poachers*, (Ashridge Press), 2001

Morris Desmond, *Dogs - The Ultimate Dictionary of over 1000 Dog Breeds*, (Ebury Press), 2001

Morrison, Robert, *The Individuality of the Pig: It's Breeding, Feeding and Management*, (E. P Dutton & Company), 2012

Niall, Ian, *The New Poachers Handbook*, (William Heinemann Ltd), 1960

Peach, Julia, *The Origins of Poaching in Lincolnshire*, (The Lincolnshire Poacher), 2014

Poynter, Dan, *Dan Poynter's Self-Publishing Manual: How to Write, Print and Sell Your Own Book,* (Para Publishing), 2007

Ryder Haggard, Lilias, *I Walked by Night*, (Ivor Nicholson and Watson), 1946

Sheail, John, *Rabbits and their History*, (David & Charles Ltd), 1971

Tovey, Bob & Brian, McDonald, John F., The Last English Poachers, (Simon & Schister Ltd), 2015

Willock, Colin, *Kenzie The Wild Goose Man,* (Harper Collins), 1972

Websites

Briggs, Stacia and Connor, Siofra, *Eleuminated Owl*, (Eastern Daily Press), https://www.edp24.co.uk/news/weird-norfolk-mysterious-luminescent-glowing-barn-owls-norfolk-1232400 23/01/21

Complete Jewish Bible, *Proverbs 30 V.26*, (Bible Gateway), https://www.biblegateway.com/passage/?search=Proverbs+30%3A26-28&version=CJB 11/01/21

Cohen, Tamara, *An apple a day keeps the doctor away (especially if it's an old variety)*, (Associated Newspapers Ltd), https://www.dailymail.co.uk/health/article-2128310/An-apple-day-keeps-doctor-away-especially-old-variety.html 15/02/21

Cryer, Pat, *The Victorian Kitchen Range*, (webmaster.cryer), https://www.1900s.org.uk/1900s-cooking-range.htm 15/02/21

Editorial Team, *Allium Ursinum: Our Native Wild Garlic*, (The Oldie), https://www.theoldie.co.uk/blog/allium-ursinum-our-native-wild-garlic 21/01/21

Editorial Team, *Black Act Laws and Man Traps,* (Godalming Museum), http://www.godalmingmuseum.org.uk/index.php?page=man-trap 11/01/21

Editorial Team, Cliff, *Lincolnshire Poacher Rose*, (Help Me Find) https://www.helpmefind.com/rose/l.php?l=2.33891.0 27/01/21

Editorial Team, *Games Laws*, (Encyclopedia Britannica 1911), https://theodora.com/encyclopedia/g/game_laws.html 22/01/21

Editorial Team, *International Lincolnshore Poacher Speedtrack Racing*, (Super Speedtrack), http://www.superspeedtrack.com/poacher.html 28/01/21

References

Editorial Team, *Lincolnshire Poacher - Metheringham*, (Facebook), https://www.facebook.com/TheLincolnshirePoacherInn/ 11/01/21

Editorial Team, *Lincolnshire Poacher - Nottingham*, (Castlerock Brewery), https://www.castlerockbrewery.co.uk/pubs/lincolnshire-poacher/ 11/01/21

Editorial Team, *Lincolnshire Poacher, Spalding*, (Facebook) https://www.facebook.com/The-Lincolnshire-Poacher-148279375296758/ 11/01/21

Editorial Team, *Operation Galileo*, (Grantham Matters), https://www.granthammatters.co.uk/police-launch-this-years-operation-galileo-to-tackle-hare-coursers/ 11/01/21

Editorial Team, *RNLI Lifeboat Lincolnshire Poacher*, (RNLI), http://www.rnliskegness.org.uk/information/50/past+lifeboats/ 28/01/21

Editorial Team, *Slenderman*, (Friends of Lincoln Castle), http://www.folc.co.uk 28/01/21

Editorial Team, *The Poacher's Companions*, (The Vintage Gun Journal), https://www.vintageguns.co.uk/magazine/the-poacher-s-companion 22/01/21

Editorial Team, *The Poacher Line*, (Facebook), https://www.facebook.com/poacherline/ 11/01/21

Gosling, Dennis, *Lincolnshire Poacher - Bunkers Hill*, (Marstons), https://www.lincolnshirepoacherpub.co.uk 11/01/21

HM Government, *The Ground Games Act 1880*, (Eyre and Spottiswoode on behalf of HM Goverment), https://www.legislation.gov.uk/ukpga/1880/47/pdfs/ukpga_18800047_en.pdf 27/01/21

Jones, Laurence, *North Kesteven Coat of Arms*, (Heraldry-wiki), https://www.heraldry-wiki.com/heraldrywiki/wiki/Lincolnshire_-_Parts_of_Kesteven 02/02/21

King James Bible, *Psalms 104 V18*, (Bible Hub), https://www.biblehub.com/psalms/104-18.htm 11/01/21

Read, F.W. & Sons, *Lincolnshire Poacher Cheese*, (FW Read & Sons Ltd), https://lincolnshirepoachercheese.com 11/01/21

Site Contributor, Malsfotofile, *Lincolnshire Poacher Spalding*, (Smugmug), https://malsfotofile.smugmug.com/Other-4/Lincolnshire/i-FDFLhpJ/A 11/01/21

Swift, Jonathan, *Rabbits Old and Rabbits New Grace*, (The Free Library), https://www.thefreelibrary.com/It%27s+good+to+say+Grace.-a0390027646 02/02/21

The Lincolnshire Poacher

Unknown, *The Goose and The Common,* (Union Songs - Mark Gregory), http://unionsong.com/u765.html 03/03/21

Wikipedia Contributors, *Lincolnshire Poacher,* (Wikipedia, The Free Encyclopedia), https://en.wikipedia.org/wiki/The_Lincolnshire_Poacher 11/01/21

Wikipedia Contributors, *Lincolnshire Poacher Numbers Station,* (Wikipedia, The Free Encyclopedia), https://en.wikipedia.org/wiki/Lincolnshire_Poacher_(numbers_station) 11/01/21

Wikipedia Contributors, *Lincolnshire Spinach,* (Wikipedia, The Free Encyclopedia), https://en.wikipedia.org/wiki/Blitum_bonus-henricus 11/01/21

Pictures

Abel, Keith, *Roast Pigeons with Wild Mushrooms and Sage,* (Abel and Cole Ltd), https://www.abelandcole.co.uk/recipes/roast-pigeon-with-wild-mushrooms--sage 11/02/21

Archer, Fred, *Poacher's Pie,* (Hodder and Stoughton Paperbacks), 1976

Briggs, Stacia and Connor, Siofra, *Eleuminated Owl,* (Eastern Daily Press), https://www.edp24.co.uk/news/weird-norfolk-mysterious-luminescent-glowing-barn-owls-norfolk-1232400 23/01/21

Cliff, *Lincolnshire Poacher Rose,* (Help Me Find), https://www.helpmefind.com/rose/l.php?l=2.33891.0 27/01/21

Cuthbert, Robert, Eastham, Jake and Parle, Andy, *A Hunter's Step-by-Step Guide to Cooking Game,* (Hermes House, Anness Publishing Ltd), 2010

de Bruin, Eveline, *Fox,* (Pixabay), https://pixabay.com/photos/fox-predator-mammal-wild-fauna-1682882/ 22/01/21

Editorial Team, *Bacon, Leek and Mushroom Suet Pudding,* (Scullerymaidsblog), http://scullerymaidsblog.com/2014/bacon-leek-mushroom-suet-pudding/ 11/02/21

Editorial Team, *Braised Rabbit and Apple Stew,* (stuartsdinners), https://stuartsdinners.wordpress.com/about/ 11/02/21

Editorial Team, *International Lincolnshire Poacher Speedtrack Racing,* (Super Speedtrack), http://www.superspeedtrack.com/poacher.html 28/01/21

Editorial Team, *John Wesley Biography,* (TheFamousPeople), https://www.thefamouspeople.com/profiles/john-wesley-88.php 18/01/21

Editorial Team, *Kenzie Thorpe,* (East Anglian Film Archive), http://www.eafa.org.uk/catalogue/330 27/01/21

References

Editorial Team, *Kenzie Thorpe,* (South Holland Heritage), https://www.heritagesouthholland.co.uk/article/mackenzie-thorpe-poacher-gooseman/ 27/01/21

Editorial Team, *King George IV*, (Brighton Museums), https://brightonmuseums.org.uk/royalpavilion/history/who-was-george-iv/ 04/02/21

Editorial Team, *Longnetting - Rabbit Control in Wiltshire*, (Wiltshire Warreners), http://www.wiltshirewarreners.co.uk/page/long-netting.php 30/01/21

Editorial Team, *MacFie's Treacle Tin*, (Worthpoint.com), https://www.worthpoint.com/worthopedia/macfies-black-treacle-candy-tin-238561682 22/01/21

Editorial Team, *Pignuts*, (Wild Food UK), https://www.wildfooduk.com/edible-wild-plants/pignut/ 25/02/21

Editorial Team, *Rabbiting Spade*, (Worthpoint.com), https://www.worthpoint.com/worthopedia/vintage-antique-rabbiting-poaching-1657428873 23/02/21

Editorial Team, *Operation Galileo,* (Grantham Matters), https://www.granthammatters.co.uk/police-launch-this-years-operation-galileo-to-tackle-hare-coursers/ 11/01/21

Editorial Team, *Rabbit Pie*, (Eynsham Parish Council), https://eynsham-pc.gov.uk/org-news.aspx?nid=537 11/02/21

Editorial Team, *Rev. Canon Alan Robson,* (Methodist Church Lincoln), http://lincolnmethodist.org.uk/rev-canon-alan-robson/ 23/01/21

Editorial Team, *RNLI Lifeboat Lincolnshire Poacher*, (RNLI), http://www.rnliskegness.org.uk/information/50/past+lifeboats/ 28/01/21

Editorial Team, *Rock Salt Cartridges - The Box O'Truth,* (Carbon Media Group Outdoors), https://www.theboxotruth.com/the-box-o-truth-33-rock-salt-in-a-shotgun/ 22/01/21

Editorial Team, *Smithfield Sheepdog History*, (sites.google.com), https://sites.google.com/site/smithfieldsheepdog/home/smithfield-history 23/02/21

Editorial Team, *Sorrel*, (The Spruce), https://www.thespruce.com/how-to-grow-sorrel-4121351 11/02/21

Editorial Team, *The Poacher Line*, (Poacherline.org), https://poacherline.org.uk 03/02/21

Editorial Team, *Tic Beans,* (Chase Wildlife), https://chasewildlife.co.uk/shop/wildlife-feeds/straight-feeds/tic-beans-pigeon-feed/ 22/01/21

The Lincolnshire Poacher

Editorial Team, *Whisperer in Darkness - Lovecraft Investigations*, (BBC), https://www.bbc.co.uk/sounds/play/p07wgmh0 04/02/21

Flickr Contributor 6089Gardener, *Lincolnshire Poacher Steam Train*, (Flickr), https://www.flickr.com/photos/60539035@N02/50008674932/in/photolist-2jc6wMj-WTB3AN-CyR6Lr-27iPZdo-272DoYD-28jZ2W5-25DmKZW-ydLUdR-JKnCrt-7CGksK-28pjuRK-LCci7B-25DmJn7-LgrwJw-27iPWNJ-LgrxFw-omEN3U-25DmHCw-27iPVpG-bnaeWY-25DmvFq-bAafAc-cSYzKG-25DmLVJ-27iPUhS-puHFr9-28jZb97-24ywMg4-JKnJAn-Lgryks-28pjwsR-272DGuk-LgruVw-25Dmyiu-fDrD82-2f6ojBb-25DmwwJ-24ywMbp-27iPR6w-JKnEkt-LgrowQ-LgrdLs-ojQTnq-28pjqdM-27iPwG7-27iPwnu-M2avz7-Cu2TD4-JKnxz4-LgrmgC 03/02/21

Frankland-Payne-Gallwey, Sir Ralph, *Plan of Decoy with 5 Pipes,* (Wikipedia, The Free Encyclopedia), https://commons.wikimedia.org/w/index.php?curid=37228566 22/01/21

Frankland-Payne-Gallwey, Sir Ralph, *Decoyman Enticing Wild Ducks up the Decoy Pipe by the Use of a Dog*, (Wikipedia, The Free Encyclopedia), https://commons.wikimedia.org/w/index.php?curid=37228569 22/01/21

Hrohmann 5467204, *Hare*, (Pixabay), https://pixabay.com/vectors/hare-rabbit-silhouette-animal-fur-5467204/ 02/21/21

Jones, Laurence, *North Kesteven Coat of Arms*, (Heraldry-wiki), https://www.heraldry-wiki.com/heraldrywiki/wiki/Lincolnshire_-_Parts_of_Kesteven 02/02/21

Love Antiques Contributors, *Osmonds & Sons Label*, (LoveAntiques), https://www.loveantiques.com/items/listings/vintage-osmond-son-ltd-stock-owners-medicine-chest-pine-storage-box-LA189261 03/02/21

Marston, Silvanus, *The New Poachers Handbook*, (William Heinemann Ltd), 1960

Meridian Meats, *Lincolnshire Stuffed Chine,* (Slow Food in the UK), https://www.slowfood.org.uk/ff-products/lincolnshire-stuffed-chine/ 17/02/21

Middleton, Alan, *Draining the Fens,* (County Life Ltd), https://www.lincolnshirelife.co.uk/posts/view/draining-the-fens 12/02/21

References

Momentmal 2520646, *Binoculars*, (Pixabay), https://pixabay.com/photos/binoculars-old-nostalgia-distant-2520646/ 23/01/21

Moore, Peter, *Alarm Gun*, (Executors of Peter Moore's Will), 04/09/2020

Moule, Thomas, *Map of Lincolnshire*, (Thomas Moule c1842/ Wrightsons Foilgraphics London)

Philipallan, *Royal Game Soup*, (Immediate Media Company Ltd), https://www.bbcgoodfood.com/user/616230/recipe/royal-game-soup 11/02/21

Picclick Contributors, *Osmonds White Oils*, (Picclick), https://picclick.co.uk/Giant-cobalt-blue-Osmonds-White-Oil-Veterinary-233795484266.html#&gid=1&pid=2 13/01/21

Shaw, Hank, *Rabbit in Mustard Sauce*, (Dotdash), https://www.simplyrecipes.com/recipes/rabbit_in_mustard_sauce/ 11/02/21

Spall, A.V., *Poacher Paintings - Various, (featured at the end of some chapters)* Provided by John Larder (deceased)

Stainbrook, Dorothy, *Pheasant Normandy Stew with Apples, Cream and Onions*, (HeathGlen Farm and Kitchen), https://farmtojar.com/pheasant-normandy-stew-with-apples-cream-onions/#:~:text=%20Ingredients%20%201%204- 11/02/21

Westcott, Andrew, *An Introduction to British Made Steel Gin Traps*, (QSL.net), https://www.qsl.net/2e0waw/gintraps.htm 30/01/21

Wikipedia Contributors, *Ransoms*, (Wikipedia, The Free Encyclopedia), https://en.wikipedia.org/wiki/Allium_ursinum#/media/File:Allium_ursinum0.jpg 11/01/21

The Lincolnshire Poacher

*He did rise from his roost,
Checking his female companions.*

Index

A
Anderson, Bill 60
Australia 34, 77, 128
   Maitland 34
   New South Wales 34

B
Barton, Lord Billy the Hat 5
Beaters xii, 115
Bembridge, C. L. 74
Bible 32, 36
   Proverbs 32
Billingborough 13
Billinghay 66
Bird Calls 21
Bletchley Park 107
Boston 13, 39, 70, 103
Brace 115
Brighouse and Rastrick Brass Band 108, 120
Britten, Benjamin 108
Buzzard 35

C
Callsigns 74
Cartridges 24, 26, 27, 28
Cat 9
Catapult 16, 64, 65
Churchill, Winston 72
Clarke, William 45, 50, 56, 58, 59
Cleethorpes 104
Coal 39
Cobbett, William 4
Colman's Mustard Powder 88, 89, 120
Coningsby 1, 2, 32, 71
Count, Alan 63, 64
Countryside Alliance 120
County Magazine 111, 121
Cranwell 107
Curlew 77

D
Deer 27, 116
Deportation 43, 44, 45, 57
Dog 5, 6, 7, 8, 12, 13, 19, 43, 59
   Bedlington 7
   Border Terrier 5, 12
   Decoy Dogs 6, 13
   Greyhound 7
   Lincolnshire Longdog 7, 39
   Lurcher 7, 39
   Norfolk Terrier 5
   Saluki 7
   Setter 126
   Smithfield-Drover 7, 8
Dogdyke 1
Dowse, John 74
Duck 11, 12, 13, 37
   Eider 37
   Mallard 37, 37–42, 77
Duck Decoy 11, 12, 13, 37
   Spider Dykes 12

E
East Anglian Film Archive 78, 120
East Midlands Railway 103, 120
Eggs 9, 41
Egremont Russet Apples 85
Epworth 2
Ermine 112
Eyesight 69, 70

F
Farm
   Cold Harbour 1
   Hungry Hill 1
   No Man's Friend 1
   Toft Hill 71, 72
   Warren 1
Farmers xiii, xiv, 60
Fens 2, 11, 17, 33, 60, 66, 67, 69, 77

Ferret 8, 20, 21, 76, 116
  Pine Martin 8
  Polecat 8
Film & TV
  Lovecraft Investigations 109
  Tom Brown's School Days 109
  Truth Seekers 109
Fish 40, 93
  Pike 41, 93
  Salmon 40
  Trout 40, 41
Five Mile House 68
Fogarty's 13
Folklore xiv
Forcemeat 116
Fox 6, 65
Fulsby Wood 71

G

Gamechips 116
Gamekeeper xiii, xiv, 9, 11, 17, 18, 22, 33, 41, 63, 64, 65, 66, 69, 72, 73, 74, 78, 121
Game Laws xi, 40, 44
  Black Act 43
  Ground Game Act 34
Ganzie 76, 116
GCHQ 74
Geese 11, 12, 27, 77
Gibraltar 128
Glow-worms 66, 67
Gold 69, 70
Goldsmith, Oliver 33
Grantham 103
Grasstrack 113, 123
Groundswell 120, 126
Guns 23, 24, 25, 27, 77
  7mm Luger 71, 72
  12 Bore 23, 28, 70, 74
  .410 24, 25, 26, 39, 71, 75
  Boss & Co 25, 120
  Cartridges 27, 70
  Churchill's 25, 120
  Elderkins 25, 26, 120
  Holland & Holland 25, 120
  Lee Enfield .303 Rifle 25
  MGR Guns 121, 127
  Purdey's 25, 122
  Rock Salt 28
  Vintage Gun Journal 25, 122
  Webley & Scott 27, 123

H

Hare xii, 7, 10, 20, 31, 35, 36, 39, 60, 61, 77, 35, 86, 91
Hare Coursing xii, 35, 61
Harris, Phil 108
Hatfield, Miss S 32
Hedge-planting 35
Hen Harriers 35
Horncastle 60
Humphries, John 76, 78

I

Imperial War Museum 120
IXL Knives 121

J

Jack O'Lantern 67
Jekyll, Gertrude 43
Jerborams, Malachi 68
Jones, Marc 61

K

Kingfisher 9, 18
King George IV 108
Kirkstead Abbey 125
Kitchen Range 95, 96
Kites 35
Knitting Needle 15
Kyme, North and South 2

L

Labour in Vain 1
Landowners xi, xii, xiii, 11, 17, 34, 35, 40, 41, 43, 73, 74, 78
Langdale, George W.T. 113
Lawrence, D.H. 64
Lincoln 32, 39, 44

Index

Lincoln Castle 44, 45, 46, 58, 59, 121
   Prison 44
Lincoln Heath 32
Lincolnshire Poacher Cheese 94, 121
Lincolnshire Sausage 57, 58
Lincolnshire Spinach 42, 70
Lincolnshire Stuffed Chine 95
London 13, 33, 39
Long Sutton 76
Louth Park 33, 34
Lutein 69, 70

M

Mablethorpe, Neil 28
Martin 28
Military
   20th Battalion, Australian Imperial Force 107
   81st Regiment of Foot (Loyal Lincoln Volunteers) 107
   Bletchley Park 119
   GCHQ 120
   Intelligence Corps 107
   Lincoln and Welland Regiment 107
   New York Regiments 107
   Royal Anglian Regiment 104, 105, 119
   Royal Lincolnshire Regiment 105, 107
Mills, Derek 76, 78
Myxomatosis 32, 82, 117

N

National Farming Union 60, 121
Netting 19, 20, 112, 116, 117
   Bagging 115
   Clap Net 116
   Drag Net 116
   Funnel Net 116
   Gate Net 19, 20
   Long Net 19, 117
   Purse Net 19, 20, 117
   Trail Net 19

Norfolk 5, 6, 7, 67
North Kesteven 112, 121
Norton Disney 49, 58
Nottingham 39, 58, 101, 103, 104
Number Stations 107, 108, 109

O

Operation Galileo 60
Osmond's White Oils 75, 76, 122

P

Partridge xii, 9, 19, 36, 77, 81, 83
   Red Leg 36
Pea and Horsehair 14
Peace, Charles 63, 64, 65, 66, 127
Penknife 16
Peter Moore 43
Pheasant xii, xiii, 9, 13, 14, 15, 17, 27, 29, 31, 38, 39, 60, 65, 71, 73, 74, 75, 77, 81, 83, 85, 73
Phloridzin 85
Phosphorous Owl 66, 67
Pig 3, 4, 27, 28, 70, 72, 126
   Lincolnshire Curly Coat 3, 95
Pigeon 40, 84, 87
Poacher Line 103
Pole Vault 17
Police and Crime Commissioner 122
Police Officers xiii, 15, 29, 60, 61, 127
POW 73
Protean Behaviour 6, 12
Pubs
   Bunkers Hill 98
   Louth 102
   Metheringham 100
   Nottingham 101, 103
   Spalding 99
   Stamford 102
   Strugglers Inn 59
   White Bull 2

R

Rabbit xii, 5, 6, 7, 8, 9, 15, 16, 19, 20, 21, 31, 32, 33, 34, 35, 68, 73, 75, 76, 80, 81, 82, 88, 89, 90, 96, 112, 117
  Common Grey 33
  Coneys 32, 116
  Conies 32, 45, 48, 116
  Silverback 33, 34
Rabbiting Spade 21
Radio Lincolnshire 108, 119, 127
RAF 107, 122
  RAF Digby 74
Rationing 32, 33
Reckitt 122
RNLI 122
  Lifeboat 112, 113
Rose 113
Roud Folk Song Index 105, 122
Russia 74
Rutland 105

S

Scaman, Stanley 42
Scarborough, Dennis 72
Sheffield 16, 75
Shelduck 77
Shutknife 16
Silverback 33
Skegness 103
Skinner, Edwin 28, 29
Sleaford 2, 103
Slenderman 56, 58, 59
Snare 15, 16, 116, 117
  Slip Snare 117
Sorrel 87, 93
Spalding 25
St Pancras 104
Sugar Beet 39
Sulphur 70
Supermarkets xii
Surrey 43
Swan 77
Swift, Jonathan 68

T

Tattershall Bridge 2
Taylor's Eye Witness 122
Theddlethorpe 42
Thorpe, Kenzie 76, 77, 78
Tic Beans 29
Timberland 28, 74
Train 104
Traps 18
  Dog Spears 43
  Fenn Trap 116
  Gin Trap 18, 116
  Man Trap 18, 43, 117
  Pole Trap 18
  Spring Guns 43, 117
Twain, Mark 28

U

Unite 121

V

Van Geest, Lucille 113
Vernon, Michael 113
Virginia 57, 128

W

Wainfleet 113
Walcott 28
Wall Street Journal 63, 65, 123, 127, 129
Warren 5, 6, 33
Waterside 3, 74
Wesley, John 2, 121
Wigeon 77
Willock, Colin 78
Will O' The Wisp 67
Witham, River 2, 68
Woodhall Spa 71, 125, 127
  1940's Festival 5, 123
Woolwich 48, 57

Y
Yellowbellies xiv, 117

Z
Zeaxantin 69, 70

The Lincolnshire Poacher

*He scented a disturbance
So away he did dash.*

Lightning Source UK Ltd.
Milton Keynes UK
UKHW050708210122
397469UK00006BA/198